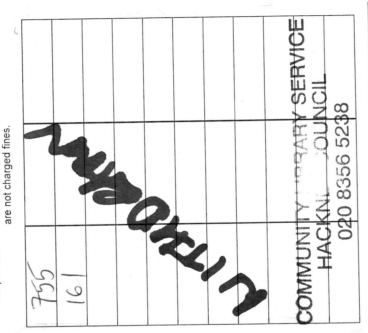

EMELI SANDÉ

THE BIOGRAPHY

EMELI SANDÉ

THE BIOGRAPHY

DAVID NOLAN

JOHN BLAKE

Published by John Blake Publishing Ltd,
3 Bramber Court, 2 Bramber Road,
London W14 9PB, England

www.johnblakepublishing.co.uk

www.facebook.com/johnblakepub **facebook**
twitter.com/johnblakepub **twitter**

First published in hardback in 2013

ISBN: 9781782194613

British Library Cataloguing-in-Publication Data:
A catalogue record for this book is available from the British Library.

Design by www.envydesign.co.uk

Printed in Great Britain by CPI Group (UK)

1 3 5 7 9 10 8 6 4 2

© Text copyright David Nolan, 2013

Papers used by John Blake Publishing are natural, recyclable products made from wood grown in sustainable forests. The manufacturing processes conform to the environmental regulations of the country of origin.

To Helen, Ian and everyone at Title Role
Productions for teasing me out of TV retirement.
It's all your fault.

AUTHOR BIOGRAPHY AND ACKNOWLEDGEMENTS

David Nolan is a multi award-winning journalist who has written for newspapers, magazines, radio and television. He's made television documentaries about bands from the Sex Pistols to The Smiths and authored biographies on Ed Sheeran, Simon Cowell and Tony Wilson.

Thanks to Muslim Alim, John Ansdell (www.innovationmusic.co.uk), Megan Ansdell (www.nightowlimaging.co.uk), Mel Awasi, Richard Bull, David Craig, Yasmin Evans, Laura McCrum, Lucian Randall, Mark Robb (www.starlarecords.com), Clare Tillyer and Jeff Zycinski – an A to Z of assistance.

Throughout the interviews for this book, many of the people who kindly gave me their time constantly referred to the person that you and I know as Emeli Sandé as 'Adele' – it's her real name after all. Adele Sandé is the person they know. In this version of events – to save confusion – I've stuck with Emeli.

Contents

INTRODUCTION – London 2012 ix

ONE – Donside Welcomes African Teacher 1

TWO – An Urban Scot 17

THREE – Have You Heard the Lost Album? 37

FOUR – Her Name is Rio 57

FIVE – Let the Writing Commence 69

SIX – A Massive Attack on the Charts 87

SEVEN – We're Gonna Do It How We Do It 109

EIGHT – They Didn't Know I Was in Both 129

NINE – The Montenegrin Daughter-in-Law 155

TEN – If I Don't Party Tonight....
    Then I'll Never Party 175

ELEVEN – Music For Grannies? 199

TWELVE – Discography, DVDs, key songwriting
    credits and collaborations 223

Introduction
London 2012

The pulse of what sounds like a human heartbeat is the only introduction that the former medical student is given – and it is all that she appears to need. With the backdrop of a huge bell, she begins to sing.

Beneath her, a troupe of dancers is moving beneath the buzzing glow of a huge, orange orb. The dance they are performing represents mortality. They throw dust into the air as they move – the dust has been specially chosen so it dissipates through the air at just the right speed. There are 52 dancers in all – including a ten-year-old boy and choreographer Akram Khan – and the number is no coincidence. It's to pay tribute to the 52 people killed in the 7/7 London bombings in 2005.

The song she is singing – 'Abide With Me' – is a hymn, based on a poem written by a man facing his own death with quiet resignation: the Reverend Henry

Francis Lyte. The hymn has become a staple of British sporting events since it was written in 1847. It meant a great deal to the singer too: it had been played at her grandad's funeral.

It's a hymn written by a Scot, being sung by an adopted Scot at the opening ceremony of the Olympic Games in London. 'You've got to pay tribute to her,' Danny Boyle, the director of the event, said of the singer's choice. 'Because to sing solo, unaccompanied, with nothing to help you... that is an incredible achievement. That woman's voice is just... we were very proud of that. That was our high art moment.'

The song may have been a traditional one, but the singer's way of acknowledging was perfectly modern: 'Wow, so many amazing msgs,' she tweeted. 'Thank you all!! That was the most incredible experience of my life, so proud to be a part of London 2012.'

Her slot at the opening of the games – and her accidental double-booking for the closing ceremony in two weeks time – introduced her to a global audience, although some viewers didn't get to see 'Abide With Me' until later. The performances gave her the momentum to shift her career and her sales into the stratosphere.

Emeli Sandé's rise to this moment seemed to have been a flawless one.

Easy.

But that wouldn't be a true or complete version of the events that had brought her to this point.

One

Donside Welcomes African Teacher

Though her heritage is diverse and the people of Scotland claim her as their own, Adele Emeli Sandé is a Mackem. That's the slang term for someone born in Sunderland in the northeast of England. It's believed the expression comes from Sunderland's shipyards where they used to 'make 'em' – build the ship structures – before they were fitted out in Newcastle. They were the creators who put together the great constructions admired by so many.

Don't confuse Mackems with Geordies. Neither side of the Sunderland/Newcastle divide will thank you for that. There's a long-standing rivalry between the two cities but it's all part of the friendly banter that's characteristic of the area. Less so the reaction Emeli's white mother and black father got in some quarters when they first met. 'In the '80s my parents were in Sunderland and they went through some awful things,' she later explained in an interview with the *Daily Mail*. 'They have some awful stories. They got people saying things to them in the streets, in bars. It was tough for them.'

Emeli was born on 10 March 1987 when the UK No 1 single was a gently reggaefied version of 'Everything I Own' by Boy George. Twenty-six years later, the former Culture Club singer would approach Sandé at a Prince's Trust charity event and tell her how much he liked her new single, a song called 'Next to Me'.

Sandé's family on her mother's side are from the other side of the country – the northwest of England. Emeli's mum, Diane Wood, is a Cumbrian and grew up in the Smithfield area of Egremont. This market town is best known for its annual crab fair and gurning competition, in which competitors try to pull the worst face possible to win the title of champion. Diane lived in Old Smithfield and attended Whitehaven grammar school before heading over to Sunderland to attend the city's polytechnic. It was on the Sunderland campus that Diane met Joel Sandé in 1984. Family legend has it that Joel approached Diane with the following immortal chat-up line: 'Hi, I'm Sandé... like the day of the week.'

'It worked,' Emeli recalled, 'and some 25 years on they're still together.'

It's hard to imagine a more contrasting back story to her mother's than that of Emeli's father Joel: 'My dad is from Zambia and is a very focused man,' Emeli later explained to Scotland's *Herald* newspaper. 'He has a very great mind actually. He was one of the cleverest people in his country, he went to a special school, he came to England. He is very focused and he always made it clear to me that education is very important and that you have a responsibility to achieve something and make something of your life. And that was very important to them. And my mum as well. They were both the first people in their families to go to university.'

The importance placed on education in the Sandé family was something that would make one of the key decisions in her life – the choice between continuing her university degree or pursuing a career in music – a very difficult one. 'In my family,' she later explained to journalist Lucy Gannon, 'we grew up with a huge respect for education instilled in us.'

Joel Sandé had arrived at Sunderland thanks to the sponsorship of the Zambia Consolidated Copper Mines – a deal only offered to the best of the best. He had come to Britain to study mechanical engineering. The intention was always to get his degree and return to Zambia, but the plan changed when he met Diane

Wood. The pair married in 1986 and Emeli was born just as the young couple were finishing their degrees. 'I don't think people in the northeast then were used to the idea of a mixed marriage,' Joel later revealed in an interview for the *Sunday Times*. 'We were in education circles and the students accepted it but if we went out I wouldn't say it was a happy experience. People would say things, and Diane wouldn't always understand the situation – it was just better to ignore them. We eventually learnt to ignore the comments because otherwise it would have meant me fighting every person I met in the street, which wouldn't have been healthy.'

When Emeli was aged just one, the Sandés decided to leave the UK and headed for Zambia. It was to be a short-lived taste of African life; Diane became ill with malaria at the same time as she became pregnant with Emeli's sister, Lucy, and returned to England with Emeli to be closer to her family in Cumbria. It would be two long years until Joel was able to follow them, a terrible separation for a young family.

When he arrived back in the UK Joel found it hard to get work in the engineering sector and decided to retrain as a teacher. There would be more separation, as the university place he got was in Aberdeen in Scotland, more than 300 miles away. It wasn't until Joel got a posting to a school in Alford, a village west of Aberdeen, that the family was reunited. 'I'd wanted to work somewhere in the countryside because I knew Diane would be happier there,' Joel later explained to journalist Matt Munday. 'Someone mentioned to me that when I first walked into Alford you could hear a pin drop. But everybody had been informed there was going to be an African teacher coming into the village, so it was a bit of a novelty for a while, but they were very accepting.'

Joel's arrival in Alford – a quiet village on the banks of the River Don – was covered by the local paper: DONSIDE WELCOMES AFRICAN TEACHER said the headline. 'A new face on the staff of Alford Academy this term is Joel Sandé,' reported the *Deeside Piper*. 'He has joined the technical department and has found a warm welcome from staff and pupils alike.' The article went on to add: 'Now his wife has arrived from Cumbria and his daughter is settled in primary two in the village, he looks forward to a happy future in the village.'

The Sandés' experience in Alford would be a very different one from Sunderland. 'As a family we experienced nothing negative, nor did I encounter bullying or racism, despite being both the youngest pupil and the only black one until my sister Lucy, who's two years younger, joined me at school,' Emeli later told the *Daily Mail*. 'We were made totally welcome.'

Emeli's parents' relationship – and the story of their struggle to be accepted – would be a theme that would inspire one of the standout songs from her breakthrough album *Our Version of Events*: 'Mountains'. 'The whole song is about really finding something you're going to stick with through everything,' she later explained to the *Sun*. 'They're from different races and from a really poor background but gave me and my sister really great opportunities in life.'

Life in Alford would prove very comfortable for the Sandés, but the surrounding area was a slightly different matter. 'People knew us in the village, but any surrounding place you'd go to, you'd become a spectacle,' Emeli later explained in an interview with the *Sunday Times*. 'People would stare and it felt like a big thing. I don't remember speaking to my dad much about it, or my mum. I knew they'd been through a lot of abuse for being a mixed-race couple in the '80s. In comparison to that, people staring wasn't that big a deal.'

Though the attention she received would make Emeli reserved and quiet in public, the Sandé daughters were told by their parents that if anyone called them a name or asked them stupid questions then the answer should be a clear and simple one: just tell them they're an idiot.

The importance of education — and the opportunities it had presented to Joel Sandé — seemed to be something that had an almost talismanic power within the family. From an early age, Emeli had a thirst for knowledge that saw her ache for school:

'Even as a primary-school kid, I hated to be ill and to miss a day because I was so hungry to learn,' she later explained to the *Daily Mail*. 'I was very shy, nerdy and extremely well-behaved.'

The shyness evaporated when Emeli was back at home. Her extrovert father's influence was the key and the house was filled with music. Emeli played recorder and clarinet and also took piano lessons, making swift enough progress for her parents to buy her a piano. 'People definitely knew we were there,' she said, describing the atmosphere at home in an interview with the *Herald*. 'Quite boisterous – me singing and doing shows and my sister was loud when she was a kid. It was a loud family. [The feeling in the family was] we're all in it together, we're different and we're going to make this work. Let's get on with it. I filled up the house. It was almost like music was my secret: this is who I am.'

Although there would be phone calls and letters to relatives, Joel Sandé took the decision not to teach his daughters the language he spoke back in Zambia, believing that it wouldn't be 'useful in their education'. Words and phrases would be picked up during conversations and letters to relatives in Africa, but it appears to have been a subtle, rather than an overriding influence. 'It was definitely a part of my life: the music my dad would play, the stories he would tell and definitely the emphasis on education,'

7

she later explained to *Afripop!* magazine. 'I was definitely aware that it came from Zambia and the experiences my dad had there. So that, the whole education part of my life and expectation I felt was African and I felt very connected in that way. I have a lot of cousins that I would write to when I was younger and they are all musical. So I definitely felt like this gene within me, that I was so connected with, was from Zambia.

'I love having access to both [cultures]. When I was young I found it difficult to balance both and to be different but the older I got, the more I embraced being different and it became... it was liberating. I didn't have to fit in one box. There was no way I was ever going to fit in anywhere so it gave me this freedom to just be like, You know what? I can be who I want to be and there are no rules. So I guess that's why I love them. I've been lucky, though. My family has always been really supportive. Even though I felt different because I looked very different from my white family in the north of England, I've always been embraced by them and they always supported my music and my education.'

One thing Joel Sandé did do was share stories of their Zambian ancestors. One story in particular would stick in Emeli's mind. Joel would tell his daughter about one of his relatives back in Zambia who would get so involved in the music she was listening to, she entered a trancelike state. '[Dad] thinks I get my vocal gene from a great-aunt of his who looked after him as a child and who would suddenly go into these singing trances when she was cooking or whatever,' she later told journalist Alan Jackson. 'Apparently you couldn't stop or interrupt her until she was finished. He thinks I might be inhabited by her spirit. And while my mum's quite reserved and not as go-getting as my dad, she's a very good storyteller. I'm sure that's helped me with my songwriting.'

Emeli's sister Lucy would later paint a vivid picture of the atmosphere in the Sandé household for Scotland's *Daily Record* newspaper: 'She was always a singer. Even before school she was singing Disney songs like "The Little Mermaid". That was a particular favourite. She sang Mariah Carey songs that dad had in his record collection. I remember the house would be filled with her singing all the big ballads. Those were probably the first songs she sang and I knew how good she was, even when she was just seven years old or maybe even younger. Mum and Dad tell me that they used to tend to her crying as a baby, until they realised that she was singing.'

Emeli's mum, Diane Sandé, realised that music brought about a transformation in her daughter. 'When she was little she always loved music and performing on the recorder,' she told journalist John Dingwall. 'I noticed that it didn't bother her getting up on stage. I could see the lyrics she was writing and how deep she was going into the songwriting by the time she was 13 or 14. There was a lot of music around but I think Emeli had the music in her from the moment that she was born.'

'I was very different,' Emeli told Qtv in an interview in 2012, 'and I knew that since I was very young. There was no way of ever fitting in, there was no point trying. So I always just did my own thing. I was the weird kid with the piano. I did my own thing - the way I dressed, it was my own path. But I dreamed. I dreamed of one day moving to London, getting a record deal... but it was a dream.'

At the age of eight Emeli started to get involved with the choir and school plays at Alford Primary, something that made a real impression on her music teacher Morag Simpson. 'She was just a wee thing at that point,' Morag told the *Daily Record*. 'All the children had to play an ocarina, a South American instrument that is a wee cylinder with circles, and I taught her to play the recorder and she learned to read music. I have gone up in the estimation of the children in the schools I am teaching in now because I taught her. The kids think I am wonderful now. They are all sticking with the choir. There were lots of musical kids when I taught Emeli but she stood out as being talented enough to go on and do something with her music. I would never have guessed how far her talent would take her. I couldn't have predicted that. It is really amazing.'

At eight, Emeli also started to write her own songs: 'I don't think you could call it songwriting,' she later said, 'but it was about this alien that came from space and spread love and joy around the world. It was quite good!'

The kind of music that caught her ear and her imagination seemed to be dominated by female voices: gospel-tinged girl band Eternal were an early favourite. Big voices were a major attraction for the young Emeli: Whitney Houston and Mariah Carey. Then came more subtle artists like multi-Grammy award-winning jazz and soul singer Anita Baker – there's a great deal of Baker's timbre and phrasing in Sandé's voice. Later came deeper, broader, more socially aware artists like Tracy Chapman and Nina Simone. Simone's records came from Joel Sandé's collection and the jazz/soul singer and civil rights firebrand made a deep impression on the youngster: 'I fell in love with Nina Simone as soon as I heard her, and she really inspired me to play an instrument and to write and to speak about what's going on in the world around you.'

Joel Sandé: 'I knew when Emeli was six or seven years old that she had something special. From then on I realised she wasn't shy about making music. She tried to imitate the popular singers of the time and

11

tried to get the sound the exact same as the records. She was standing in front of a lot of people from a young age. She was happy to be heard in front of adults. She would sing Celine Dion's 'My Heart Will Go On' and she would try to reach all the notes. She sang Mariah Carey and Whitney Houston songs and later, at the age of 12, it was songs by Alicia Keys. She picked up on Nina Simone from my music collection. We played lots of different music in the house including gospel, R&B and blues.'

Gradually, the desire to perform would spread outside the house and school. She and her sister Lucy would take the songs they learned at school and sing them door to door at Halloween, with Lucy accepting her role as the backup singer. Emeli's very first solo performance was in the Alford Primary School Christmas production in 1997. 'She sang the part of Mary in [popular nativity musical] *Hosanna Rock*,' head teacher Liz MacLeod later recalled to the Sandés' local paper the *Deeside Piper*. 'She was only 10 at the time, but even then she had a voice that was remarkable. Little did I know what great things were in store for her. I did, however, keep the programme for that concert. I must have known it would be worth keeping!'

As a 10-year-old, Emeli wrote a song for a school talent show, but tellingly, chose not to perform it herself. 'Her friends performed it for her,' Liz MacLeod recalls today. 'It is amazing that she was writing songs for other people even then.'

As she prepared to go to secondary school, Emeli's shyness was still an issue. The extrovert performer at home was a very different person outside of it. In virtually every interview she has given the subject of race has come up and Sandé has gone out of her way to highlight the lack of prejudice she and her family encountered in Alford. But a girl of mixed race was not an everyday sight in the northeast of Scotland and her skin colour made her more withdrawn. 'It definitely made me more introverted, I guess,' she later told the *Daily Mail*. 'In primary school you're just a kid but when I first got to high school it was like, oh, I'm quite different. There weren't many people who enjoyed the same type of music as me. I found it very difficult to express myself or communicate.'

When Emeli moved up to secondary school at Alford Academy she was again marked out as being different from her fellow pupils. This time, however, it was for rather different reasons than she'd experienced in the past – her father Joel was a teacher at the school. 'Inevitably, throughout secondary school, it was part and parcel of my identity that I was Mr Sandé's daughter,' Emeli would later remember in an interview with the *Daily Mail*. 'No way could I muck about or get into trouble, because it would've got back to him within minutes. And Dad was strict, let me tell you… Luckily, he's also a very popular, charismatic guy. For example, he took over and revolutionised the school choir, getting it to sound good, making it a cool thing to be a part of. And, of course, I sang in it. For all that I was so studious, I'd also been writing little songs and playing recorder and clarinet from the age of four or five. It's funny to think that I was so shy, barely able to speak to adults or make a sound in public, yet became this totally other, more outgoing person when music was around.'

As her confidence grew, any opportunity to perform was grabbed with both hands. At the age of 12 she entered a council-run talent show held in Inverurie, a larger town than Alford and closer to the city of Aberdeen. At the competition, which was held at Inverurie Town Hall, she sang 'Cabaret', made famous by Liza Minnelli, and Mariah Carey's 'I Will Never Forget You' – grown-up songs for a 12-year-old to tackle. George Mitchell, who produced the shows for the local district council, recalls: 'I have a distinct memory of sitting there on a cold Sunday morning at her very first audition. She came in, sang and everybody held their breath as they listened to her. She commanded the hall.'

She may have commanded the hall, but she clearly didn't fully convince those present. The future Brit Award winner, Olympic Games opening and closing ceremony performer and multi-million selling artist failed to get through the first round of auditions at Inverurie Town Hall. 'We used to advise all the contestants on how they could improve their performance so we talked to Emeli, who was still known as Adele at that time,' George Mitchell later recalled in an interview with the *Daily Record*. 'She listened and took on board everything we said. She was a lovely person in every sense of the word.'

Undeterred, she returned the following year and entered the competition again, getting through the auditions this time and being awarded the chance to perform. Taking on board the comments made by the auditioning panel, she changed her choice of material to the gospel classic 'His Eye Is On The Sparrow', as well as songs by Christina Aguilera and Alicia Keys. The New York-born Keys was becoming a particular favourite of Emeli after the release of her debut album *Songs In A Minor*. Keys had scored a Top 3 UK hit with 'Fallin'' in April 2001 and it was hard to avoid the singer on TV and radio in the spring of that year. Emeli had researched Keys and could relate to her on a lot of levels: here was mixed-race young woman, a top-of-the class student and someone else who had been inspired by Nina Simone. 'A Woman's Worth' – Keys' second single – was the song young Emeli chose to sing at the Inverurie talent show the second time around.

This time, Emeli came third and bagged a cheque for £150. A good result, but not a win. Next year, she was back again, this time as part of a vocal group called Celeste, with local teenagers Nadia Donald and Lorna Routh. Celeste tackled a capella versions of 'Bridge Over Troubled Water' by Simon and Garfunkel and 'Fields of Gold' by Sting. They won and all three girls had the mathematically difficult task of splitting the £500 winnings three ways.

As Emeli's confidence grew, so did her desire to widen the audience for her performances. As a young child in Alford, she would stage musical shows at home, making her own tickets to be issued to her family. Then she moved on to entertaining the larger population of Inverurie. Now Emeli was in her teens, she wanted to try out her talents on big-city audiences. That meant Aberdeen.

One person whose path would cross with Emeli's many times over the forthcoming years remembers one of her earliest big-city public performances very well. Strolling through Aberdeen one day, Scottish DJ David Craig saw and heard something that stopped him in his tracks: 'One day there was a gala in the city centre of Aberdeen,' Craig told me. 'There was a young kid up on a float and she was singing "Killing Me Softly" by Roberta Flack. I think she was 13 or 14 at the time. She was just a kid. I remember just stopping and thinking, she's a little bit special.'

Two

An Urban Scot

David Craig was not the only person who would be stopped in their tracks by the emerging talent of the teenage Emeli Sandé. A wide range of music industry types would come in and out of her orbit over the next few years. A dizzying series of connections and coincidences would help forge the Emeli Sandé we know today. Many would help her in terms of encouragement, promotion, time, effort and even money. Some are still around Sandé to this day, but many are not. Some have never spoken about their part in her story until now.

The connections Emeli was making by her mid-teens were many and varied. Word about the young girl from Alford with the big voice was spreading – though she still kept her feet on the ground and had a part-time job at the Co-op in Alford.

After the Inverurie talent show success she began to be picked up by musical radars that operated a little further afield. She took part in showcases and competitions with radio station Choice FM – in an event called Rapology – and MTV, but it was a series of events and occurrences involving the BBC that provided the centrepiece for some of her earliest and most durable working relationships.

At the age of 15 Emeli entered an urban music talent show for the recently launched BBC3 youth channel. The show was fronted by R&B DJ Trevor Nelson and the song that she entered was called 'Nasty Little Lady.' 'My sister filmed me at the piano, doing a little rendition of a song I'd written when I was, like, 15, and we sent it in,' she told the *Herald* newspaper in 2010. 'God, it was really funny now I look back on it.'

'She took part in a talent contest for a show I did called *The Lowdown*,' Nelson later explained to the *Daily Record*. 'My producers were keen that there was an aspect of it that discovered new talent. [Radio 1 presenter] Reggie Yates hosted that part of the show for me and you had to watch the show to know about it, because it was pretty much under the radar. She was 16 and called Adele Sandé. What struck me was it was just a girl on the keyboards, sitting down Alicia Keys-style singing a song I think she wrote. I'd be lying if I told you I remembered it all. I did remember a girl called Adele.'

The veteran R&B and soul champion had forgotten about the young girl with curly hair he'd met when she was a teenager and hadn't realised she'd changed her name. 'Everybody was always telling me about how this girl Emeli Sandé was incredible. I thought, who is this girl? I completely forgot about the talent show - she had changed her name and it didn't ring a bell. Before I got her in to do a session for me at Maida Vale with Professor Green, I was speaking to Professor Green over the web and I heard her in the background. I said to Emeli, "I'm really glad to meet you." She said, "Yeah, yeah." She came into the studio a couple of weeks later and did an interview with me. The first thing she said was, "You don't remember me, do you?" And then she reminded me of the story and it was probably the single most embarrassing moment I have ever experienced on radio.'

The teenage Emeli won *The Lowdown* talent show but – hard to believe in this age of reality TV fame at all costs – the teenager turned down the prize on offer: the chance to make a record. The deal was with the now defunct Telstar label, which had a curiously mixed bag of artists on their books over the years: everyone from Victoria Beckham to Ant and Dec and The Cheeky Girls. Not the most cutting-edge of enterprises.

Dad Joel was on hand – as ever – to give his advice. 'She had to turn it down because, having read through the contract, it didn't give her enough security or longevity,' Joel later explained to the *Record* newspaper. 'It was just for one single and maybe one other after that. She needed something to fall back on.'

Emeli later told the Contactmusic website, 'I found it overwhelming. I guess there aren't many teenagers who would think going back to school was the better option, but I didn't want to be this girl desperate to be a singer with nothing else to fall back on. I never believed it could really happen to me.'

It was the first of what would appear to be a series of missed opportunities. In fact, it was the first demonstration of the Sandé instinct being proved right in the long term. 'It would have been a different story if I'd done it then,' she later told journalist Teddy Jamieson. 'I don't think I was prepared or ready. I don't think I knew who I was as a musician or as a person then.'

Emeli might not have put out a single at the age of 16, but something else came of the show that would stand her in good stead for many years. During the show she was spotted by BBC3 producer Carlton Dixon, who alerted one of his music industry contacts, Adrian Sykes, to the possibilities and potential of Adele Emeli Sandé. Sykes had already had a 20-year career in the music industry before meeting

Emeli. He'd started work at Island Records in 1983 before moving on to MCA Records. During that time he'd worked with everyone from Dannii Minogue to drum 'n' bass DJ Goldie before moving into management in 1997.

When Sykes was tipped off about this 'great girl' he assumed he was in for a swift trip across London. 'When he told me she was actually in Aberdeen, I was like, oh God, really?' Sykes later told the *Daily Record*. 'But he persuaded me to go. Danny D [aka music producer and manager Daniel Kojo Poku], a music publisher friend of mine, and I got on a plane, got a taxi from the airport to her house, met the family and sat down to this lovely little girl plinking out some tunes.'

Sandé would later admit she felt like, 'this little country girl, just sitting there at my piano' as the music industry men from London listened to her play. Adrian Sykes: 'She performed a song called "Matchstick Girl". Even at 16, she was clearly incredibly talented. She was still at school, a grade A student, just about to take her Highers (the Scottish equivalent of A Levels). She had a great determination and she was writing really good songs even then. She was just about to blossom.'

Something else added to the dynamic in the room that day: Joel Sandé – a considerable presence at the best of times – was recording everything that Sykes

21

said. 'I can recall being mortified,' Emeli later told the *Sunday Times*, 'but I knew he wanted to make sure that I wasn't being manipulated or wowed by all their talk. As soon as people walked through our door, they got the impression they couldn't mess me around, because Dad can be quite intimidating.'

Emeli's father and his video camera were a familiar sight every time she sang. From her earliest tiny gigs to the Royal Albert Hall, he would record events so they could be reviewed later on. This time, instead of recording Emeli, he was taping Adrian Sykes' performance. Joel Sandé: 'People came and schmoozed and talked about the good things and never about the downside of the industry. I wanted to make sure we could review what had been said before making any decisions. So I recorded all the meetings of the people who came over.'

Sykes says he fully appreciates why Joel Sandé was so protective of his teenage daughter. 'I can understand why he felt the need to tape those conversations,' he told the *Daily Record* in 2013. 'We were the big record company people coming up from London. Joel and Diane were brilliant with us though, incredibly courteous and welcoming. They were genuinely pleased that someone else believed in their daughter the way they did.'

Adrian Sykes returned to London with an agreement of sorts with the Sandés, but one that would require a certain amount of patience on his part. 'We made a deal with her when she was 16,' he later told music industry website hitquarters. 'But a year later she was offered the opportunity to study a degree in medicine. It was a chance to go away and get a real solid foundation in her life and if she still wanted to come back to music afterwards then she could. And if she did come back then it would be with the knowledge that if the music failed she would always have something to fall back on that would serve her well for the rest of her life. So for us her decision was a no-brainer.'

She wanted her education but she wanted her music too: a difficult balancing act for anyone to achieve. If it was inspiration the teenager needed then it would be found around this time at the Scottish Exhibition and Conference Centre (SECC) music venue in Glasgow. Joel Sandé drove his daughter the 150 miles from Alford to see her favourite singer, Alicia Keys. The experience seemed to harden her resolve: 'We sat way back in the arena, but the whole vibe of it, the way she presented herself, the way the crowd was reacting to her was exciting,' she later told the *Chicago Tribune*. 'The moment I heard her songs, I felt I was hearing an intelligent woman doing exactly what she wanted to do without compromise, and yet all these people were coming to see her. She was making a connection through her music without losing her integrity. She showed me that you could have both.'

Within a few years, Emeli would not only share a stage with Keys, she'd be writing songs with the US singer in her studio: 'Imagine that,' she later remembered in an interview with the *Sun* newspaper. 'There are over 10,000 fans at that gig – and it was me who got the chance to work with her. I would never have believed you if you told me that was going to happen.'

Emeli returned to Alford to complete her Highers. If music wasn't distraction enough, another new element entered her life at this time: Adam Gouraguine. She had become inseparable from the teenage boy from Montenegro – a few months younger than Emeli – and he would become her constant but very low-key companion. Gouraguine became a permanent fixture around the Sandés and, like Emeli, he had a passion for education: he wanted to become a marine biologist. Like Emeli's parents and her sister, Adam would become the subject of some of her best-known songs. He was also the subject of one of her least known: 'Baby's Eyes', her first full-on love song. It would be included in many of her early demos and made a strong impression on everyone that heard it.

Adam Gouraguine also seemed to fulfil a key criteria for the people – especially the men – in Emeli's life: 'I've never been the type of girl that is interested in hanging out with boys or what their opinions of me are or anything like that,' she later told The Quietus website in 2012, shortly after it had been revealed that she and Adam were engaged. 'Because what I really love is having something that is stable and that I know is [there for me] unconditionally. So it could be about my partner or it could be about my dad or my uncle. There are some great men in my life that are always there for me. What I really value in life is loyalty and stability. And that's what I wanted to write about.'

Emeli was accepted by Adam's family in Montenegro, where the pair would eventually marry in 2012. She received a gift from the Gouraguines – a gold pendant on a necklace – that she still wears to this day. 'I always wear this necklace,' she later told MTV. 'I feel like it just protects me. Sometimes on stage the light comes off it, so in pictures you see it reflecting. I wear it all the time, and it's kind of protection for me. [It's] from Montenegro. My fiancé's mother gave this to me. It's a monastery in these amazing hills and there's this little white church in the hills. This is the church.'

Emeli continued pursuing her music, opting to take a year out after leaving Alford Academy. This was seen by the Sandés as the ideal opportunity for Emeli to see if she really had what it took to be a musician. 'That was a time when the record companies did not know what to do with her,' Joel Sandé later recalled in an interview with the *Daily Record*. 'They called her down to London for showcases but time was running out. She had to make her mind up whether or not to go to university. She finally made the decision to carry on with her chosen career of medicine. We thought her music career would be sorted out during that year out but it never happened.'

'All the way through my childhood I loved school, and my dad underlined the importance of education,' Emeli later told the *Chicago Tribune*. 'I wanted to be a musician, but I also wanted a degree to give me more stability and power in my life. I just find the whole human body so fascinating, and the brain in particular, the mystery of it. I thought that it would be fun to study.'

So Emeli left the village of Alford and headed south to Glasgow University. She was about to become an Urban Scot – in more ways than one.

Emeli arrived at Glasgow University in September 2006 to study medicine. The university dates back to the 15th century – it's in the top 10 of UK universities and one of its favourite claims to fame is that it's the fourth oldest university in the English-speaking world. It has an enviable reputation for research but that didn't interest Emeli – she wanted to be a doctor. On arrival, she was pretty much unrecognisable from the Emeli we know today: 'I looked much like any medical student – conventional,' she later told the *Daily Mail*. 'You wouldn't have noticed me in the street. I had shoulder-length, brown curly hair. I didn't do make-up. As a med student you don't have time.'

The five-year medical course that she started covered physiology, pathology and microbiology, clinical medicine and surgery and anatomy. Anatomy would lead Emeli to her specialist subject: neuroscience. 'In Glasgow University you come into contact with dead human bodies in the first year and that's just to get you used to it,' she later recalled in an interview with website The Quietus. 'It's kind of like, this is what you're going to be doing for the next five year so you'd better get used to it. There is an anatomy section [within the university] and you go down a big tunnel and it's there. Thankfully people are still donating their bodies to medical research for med students to explore. And it's interesting because you feel so removed from the fact that these were once actual people… it was bizarre. A bizarre experience. I was learning from a dead body and I think the thing that brought it home to me was when we were looking at the brain, because we would be using a real brain, which would be passed round, but there was nothing there. Inside that brain there used to be dreams, ideas and thoughts, but now it was just organic. Just a piece of flesh. So that really made me think. Where did they go? Where is that person?'

Apart from its easily accessible mortuary, Glasgow had another attraction: its music scene. 'I really wanted to be a doctor but in my heart I was a musician,' she later told the *Sun*. 'Even when my parents dropped me off on the first day, they bought me a keyboard so I could chill out between my studies. My mum said, don't forget your music – so they believed in me too. I used to play in an Italian restaurant part-time and even sing at the Med School Talent Show. But spending all my time in the library or at home, I wasn't experiencing anything apart from medicine. It wasn't inspiring me.'

She also took a part in a student music show called *Honk!* – a pun-heavy version of the Hans Christian Andersen fairytale 'The Ugly Duckling'. It required Emeli to sing as well as act the part of the duckling's mother. 'I played the mum called Ida,' she later told Radio 2. 'I was better at the singing than the acting, to be fair.'

Emeli's choice of a city to study in had been a wise one. Throughout the decades the city of Glasgow has punched well above its weight, despite its inconvenient location 400 miles from the traditional UK capital of music, London. From the teenage blues pop of Lulu in the 1960s, the rock swagger of Frankie Miller and Alex Harvey, the post-punk art of Simple

Minds and the fey jangle of Altered Images and Orange Juice, to the Americana of Del Amitri, Teenage Fanclub, Texas and Travis, the city has enjoyed repeated musical highlights.

But if the city housed musical reputations, they tended to be based on indie guitar bands rather than urban sounds. When Emeli Sandé arrived in 2006, the city was in the grip of a retro vibe: the indie knees-up of The Fratellis and the Velvet Underground stylings of Glasvegas were the sounds that were bringing music journalists to the city. Something with a more soulful edge was just about peeking through – new kid on the block Paolo Nutini, who'd just released his debut album, but it was hardly an urban breakthrough.

Yet there were people out there trying their best to remedy the situation. People who believed that Scotland's untapped urban potential was ready to be harnessed and brought out into the open.

'Urban Scot' was a loose collective of DJs, musicians and like-minded souls who wanted to create an umbrella group of R&B, soul and rap artists. One of Urban Scot's leading lights was Dunblane DJ Mel Awasi: 'I wanted to make a difference to the music scene in Scotland,' he told me. 'I wanted to find out more about the way that concerts were organised. I wanted to find out if there were soul artists in Scotland. I thought, there must be talent out there.

They might sing at church or at home but they don't have the opportunities because this isn't London. It's Scotland. Talent can be anywhere, but that was part of the problem. When I first spoke to people about the idea it was like... Urban? In Scotland? Be serious!

'The place shouldn't define what comes from it. There was a group of us and we were on a mission to reach out to musicians, singers and rappers. We went to black churches in Scotland, we sent emails out – any opportunity to find talent, we were there. In 2001 we managed to get a list of urban artists in Scotland and a group of us spent a week driving round Scotland looking for these people. We had photographers and we wanted to document the scene. We went everywhere. We went to Inverness! That list just kept growing and growing.'

With a little help from a Prince's Trust grant, Urban Scot began providing development services for up-and-coming artists. They set up an online magazine – a real novelty in the days before social networking took a grip of the music scene – that featured profiles of the talent they'd spotted. They put on showcase gigs, organised photo shoots and even laid on singing coaching – all for free. Mel Awasi: 'It was never a business. I wanted to help these artists. I saw their talent and I wanted to create opportunities to showcase their skills. It was an enterprise.'

Laura McCrum, a former BBC Scotland presenter,

was also swept up in the Urban Scot mission: 'It was so exciting to us to go to Aberdeen and Inverness and find these people – not just black people – but people who loved black music,' she explained to me. 'It reaffirmed what I felt all along: white middle-class people like soul music too! You don't have to be black to like music of black origin.'

One of the artists who soon appeared on their radar was Adele Emeli Sandé. She was introduced to Urban Scot by DJ David Craig, the man who'd been stopped in his tracks several years earlier by her singing in his home city of Aberdeen. He'd spotted her again at a venue called The Lemon Tree in Aberdeen around the time she was moving south to Glasgow. 'She was always a little bit different and a little bit unique,' Craig told me. 'The Nina Simones, the Roberta Flacks have always called out to her. I don't think pop music and the mainstream ever attracted her in the slightest – although she's now the biggest selling artist in the UK. The early stuff she was doing wasn't really marketable as far as I could see. I thought that might be her downfall, there was nothing obviously marketable that a label could pick up on. She was so different.'

Mel Awasi: 'David was up in Aberdeen. David contacted me and said I've come across this amazing young artist. He said to me, she's The One. She's going to make it. David knows his music and he'd just rave

31

about her. We didn't discover her. She was a talent in her own right. We went to see her in Glasgow, where she was doing her degree. The talent was there. Anyone who met her could see that. What she needed was the exposure. And that's what we did. We got her profile on the front page of the website. We tried to give her as much coverage as possible. She was still going by the name of Adele at that stage.'

No matter how small the audience Emeli was playing to, the Urban Scot team could be sure of at least one or two attendees. 'Every gig from an early age, Joel was there with Diane with a camera, videoing everything,' said David Craig. 'I've never heard them boast or brag – they're pretty quiet – nice people from the village of Alford. They were always enthusiastic.'

Laura McCrum: 'Emeli had performed at quite a few gigs for us in Aberdeen and in Glasgow. The ultimate one for me, and I'll never ever forget it, she came to do a sound check at The Lemon Tree in Aberdeen for an Urban Scot gig. First of all she was on time – in fact, I think she was early! She must have been 18 or 19 at the time and just starting her medical degree. I was running about doing things and she sat at the piano, very quiet and she started to sing. I've never seen anything like it – the cleaners in the club who were mopping the floors stopped. Everybody stopped and sat down and listened to her sing. It sounds like such a cliché but my breath was taken away. That was the first time I'd heard her sing live. I'd only heard her on demos. To hear her sing that first time... I'll never forget it. Looking around seeing this guy leaning on his broom just... listening. It reminded me of a 1930s film. That's what it felt like.'

David Craig can also give a fascinating insight into Emeli's performance style at the time. 'She was really quiet – shy you might say – then she'd come on stage and come alive and the whole room would be enthralled by what she was doing, then she'd leave the stage without much of a word and then disappear into the shadows. The performance part was taking shape but I don't think the artist part was really there, it hadn't grown yet. You could see the raw talent was there in abundance.'

The Urban Scot team knew they had a real contender on their hands. There was one problem – the seeming reluctance of Sandé herself. Mel Awasi: 'We were saying to her, let's take this to the next level, let's push you, let's go down to London. She was saying... I'm not ready, I want to finish my degree. She was focused on completing her degree. A lot of us were saying, but you could be the next big thing! I'm not saying she wasn't hungry for it, but she focused on completing her education. In the meantime we wanted to get her as much exposure as possible.'

'She was always so grateful and so humble and

appreciated everything we did for her,' Laura McCrum told me. 'But I always felt like it wasn't enough. I wanted to be able to walk into Sony BMG and go: "Oi! You! Listen!"'

Emeli would later admit that there was still an underlying fear of putting her work out there and it getting shot down. At this stage it still seemed easier to be a student and gain her success through academic means. 'At med school you're told when to get to class, when to do stuff, what to study – everything is set out for you,' she later explained to Scottish journalist Teddy Jamieson. 'Whereas with music, how would I even get into the industry? Who would I meet? What type of music would I do? It was kind of unknown.'

Emeli became a regular face at Glasgow nightspots like Nice N Sleazy and The Arches and was particularly keen on Òran Mór, a buzzing music venue set in the refurbished Kelvinside parish church. Fittingly for Sandé, the venue's name is Gaelic for 'Big Song'. Glasgow worked its magic on the young student and the Sandé shyness began to slip away: 'Being away from home,' she told journalist Nicola Meighan, 'I grew a lot as a person.'

The Urban Scot showcases would often use higher profile singers, often from America, to tempt in an audience and put lesser-known acts such as Emeli Sandé on as supporting artists, to give them exposure. Emeli supported the likes of Guru, formerly one half of the acclaimed hip hop duo Gang Starr. The juxtaposition of American and Scottish acts caused a little confusion among some audiences. 'Singers like Emeli would be on stage singing all these soul numbers and between songs she'd chat to the audience,' recalls Mel Awasi. 'They'd be confused – the singing sounds American but when she talked she'd be chatting away in a Scottish accent. People were a wee bit confused.'

One person in the audience when Emeli supported Guru was John Ansdell, who was in the process of setting up his own local record label and was on the look out for talent. By coincidence, Emeli had posted an ad on a free classified ads website, looking for collaborators. John Ansdell replied. 'She posted an ad on Gumtree saying was looking to work with a new producer,' Ansdell told me. 'The first line in the ad was that her favourite artists were Lauryn Hill, D'Angelo and Jill Scott. They're all my favourite artists. I sent her an email back saying we should meet up. She sent me a link to her MySpace page. She had a couple of very rough demos on there and they were just incredible. Amazing, original songs. Right away you could tell she had it. I made it my mission to find the next big thing, a UK-based soul singer, because American artists just dominated the scene. The first person I came across was Emeli Sandé. Honestly. She was the first one.'

Three

Have You Heard The Lost Album?

I f you look closely at the lengthy thanks on the album *Our Version of Events* by Emeli Sandé, you will see the following message: 'John Ansdell and family – thank you for investing in my music!'

Behind these words is a story that could rank among pop music's great near misses. It's the story of a chance meeting, a showcase gig and an eight-track debut album of which the millions of people who bought *Our Version of Events* are probably unaware.

John Ansdell is a music fan from the west end of Glasgow who, by his own admission, 'can't write, can't sing, can't play any instruments'. Working in a school by day, he spent most of his pay travelling to

London several times a month to see his favourite artists. Neo soul was his favoured genre, the more diverse and jazz-influenced musical cousin of R&B exemplified by the likes of Erykah Badu and the aforementioned Lauryn Hill and Jill Scott.

Soon, just watching the artists wasn't enough – John wanted more. 'I just decided I wanted to be part of it somehow and that setting up my own label was the best way to do it,' he explained. 'I researched it for a few months then I took my idea to Business Gateway and the Prince's Trust – and they gave me lots of advice. It seemed quite simple: find some local talent, record a CD, do a launch and promote it. At the time soul wasn't doing anything in the charts. It was my favourite kind of music and I wanted to push it in the UK.'

After spotting Emeli – or Adele as John still calls her – at the Guru gig, John had gone to see her perform live again, this time at a festival gig in Glasgow's Kelvingrove Park, organised by Urban Scot, called Kelvin Groove. 'We sat in a pub for days thinking up the name,' recalls organiser Mel Awasi. 'We had three stages and it was raining. We had people from other stages walking over to our stage to listen to Emeli. Everyone who heard her just knew from the first word: this person's going to make it.'

Appearing alongside soul singer L Marie and rappers Steg G & The Freestyle Master, Emeli braved some terrible Glasgow weather to perform on the urban stage. This is how she was listed in the running order: 'Adele Sandé – 20-year-old half-English half-Zambian, soul singer, songwriter and producer. Adele thrives for performing live and delivers a confident, spine-chillingly soulful performance every time without fail; her live shows have received critical appraise throughout the country.'

Emeli's parents were, as ever, at the Glasgow festival and as usual Joel Sandé was recording events with his trusty video camera, capturing his daughter's performance so it could be studied afterwards. 'I remember speaking to her father at the Kelvin Groove festival,' recalls Mel Awasi. 'He'd been speaking to managers and producers. There was a lot of interest in her. As soon as anyone in the music industry heard her they were like, I want to work with her. But they [her parents] wanted her to continue with her degree. At one point her father was managing her. I remember one time I was speaking to her about a gig and she'd say, "Go and speak to my dad." I said, "Hang on, I'm asking you." She said, "No. Speak to my father."'

John Ansdell: 'I went to see her at the festival in Kelvingrove Park. It was chucking it down. I went along to see her there and we chatted briefly and I invited her to come round to my flat. It turned out she lived about 30 seconds from me. She came round to my flat and we talked about our favourite singers. I told her I wanted to start my own label and promote new talent. She was studying medicine at the time and doing the odd gig here and there. I really wanted to push her to record an album properly and release it and really take it up a notch.'

Despite not being terribly musical, John Ansdell had a keyboard in his flat and Emeli offered to perform one of her songs. She played 'Baby's Eyes', the song she had written about her boyfriend Adam Gouraguine. 'That night at my flat she played it on my keyboard that was hooked up to my computer,' Ansdell says today. 'She played it and it really blew me away. I recorded it the first time she did it and it was just incredible. I thought she had the potential to be absolutely huge. I could see it a mile off because I listened to that kind of music. When she was in my flat she did a few songs and she was incredible. I knew she could be on a par with my favourite artists. The first day at my flat we drew up a contract there and then – it was a really kind of spur-of-the-moment thing. I dug out the contract a few weeks ago just to have a wee look at it. It's quite funny. It's very Mickey Mouse. A lawyer didn't do it, we just made it up there and then.'

So in August 2007, Emeli Sandé became the first 'signing' to John's Souljawn Record – say 'Soul John' in a Scottish accent and you get the idea – and Sandé became a regular visitor to John's flat as they plotted and planned. David Craig: 'John's a fantastic guy with nothing but good intentions towards Emeli. He tried everything in his power to help her.'

Ansdell even put on an unusual 'gig' for her at a school where he was working: 'I was working part time at Notre Dame Primary School and I arranged a talent show for the kids. I thought it would be good for them to show off their talents and I brought Emeli in at the end to do a couple of songs. She did one of her own songs and a Mariah Carey song as well. Obviously no one knew who she was at the time, she was just starting out. Everyone knows who she is now and I say to the kids who were there, "Do you remember when I did the talent show and she was here?" But they can't remember! Some of them sort of remember a lady with an afro.'

Meanwhile, the young singer had been attracting attention elsewhere in Scotland. In 2007 it was announced there was to be a new show on BBC Radio Scotland called *Blackstreet*. The programme would give Emeli her earliest exposure. The man behind the show was BBC producer Muslim Alim: 'The head of BBC Radio Scotland, Jeff Zycinski, had asked staff to come up with new programme formats and I pitched *Blackstreet* to him, and the way I sold it was that BBC Radio Scotland had absolutely no black music input at all. The target audience for Radio Scotland is 40 plus and initially I think Jeff was worried it would be just rap music everywhere. We had to convince him it would be soul, blues, jazz and funk and address sounds from previous decades as well as contemporary stuff. The whole point of the series was to play a Nina Simone track and then play a local artist to give them the exposure.'

The new show put the word out for musical hopefuls across Scotland to send in their demos. BBC producer Richard Bull took over the day-to-day running of *Blackstreet* and was initially disappointed by the response: 'We didn't really have the R&B stuff coming in,' Bull explained to me. 'It was a bit of an uphill struggle. Plus this is Scotland six or seven years ago – there wasn't a huge amount of music-making going on.'

'The quality wasn't really up there, I have to say,' Muslim Alim told me. 'There was a deluge of artists but there wasn't a deluge of quality.' There was one demo though that stood out from the pack: 'She was calling herself Adele at the time and I remember getting this demo and thinking wow, what a voice. Amazing, amazing voice. The demo was quite rough, but that just highlighted her voice even more. I've never heard anyone in Scotland with this kind of voice. The only thing that jarred with me was that it was just voice and piano. Quite a hard sell, a brave thing to do, considering that Amy Winehouse was big at the time and *Back to Black* was everywhere. So I wasn't wholly convinced.'

Producer Richard Bull: 'We were really keen to get stuff coming in that was Scottish. Then this demo arrived – it was delivered by hand. I then got an email from Emeli's mother with all her contact details, so her mum was very much her cheerleader at the time. The demo certainly stood out vocally. It sounded like a home recording with a great vocal and a not-so-great keyboard accompaniment. It sounded like it was – an early demo by someone who hasn't got all the kit. But we got it on the show the week after we got it. This would have been at the beginning of 2007.'

The new series began to take shape and Urban Scot's Laura McCrum – who'd battled long and hard to get an urban show on BBC Scotland – was drafted in as presenter of the new show. 'I went in saying let's hit hard with well known music like Stevie Wonder and Jill Scott, but let's also feature what's going on locally on the ground and give it a platform.'

Blackstreet was given two short series – one in early 2007, the other later in the year. The show would give Emeli her first real airplay. Radio 1Xtra is usually given the credit for being the first station to get behind the young singer. Laura McCrum: 'Every time I hear that I want to say, excuse me? From the first meeting I had with Richard and Muslim there were four or five artists I really wanted to feature and one of them was Emeli.'

Emeli made two appearances on *Blackstreet* that year

and Laura McCrum remembers both well. 'She came into the studio – it was a lovely interview. She was still quite shy. We played out her tracks – we had 'Baby's Eyes' and a cover version – and we had her singing live doing an acoustic set.'

Richard Bull recalls that after Emeli's appearances there was a low-key response. 'It was before social networks,' he reminded me. 'We got some emails but the response wasn't outstanding. I had a nice correspondence with her mum though.'

I asked Richard Bull if he thought the Emeli he came across in 2007 would become a global star. 'Absolutely not. And that's no reflection on her. But I would never have imagined that an R&B singer with her mum acting on her behalf from Aberdeenshire would have achieved this. It's like a fairy-tale, isn't it? When we got the demo, it was nice song... nice voice... but you never would have thought, this is going to be the biggest selling artist of 2012. It's funny that now she has this reputation for always getting the good gigs – the Olympics, for example – it's fitting that back then she was right on the ball. There were these R&B programmes on BBC Scotland: she was on the ball, her mum was on the ball, they were positive and proactive and they provided us with good material that was perfect for the programme. That's what she's gone on to be, isn't it? She's always perfect for the time and for events as they've unfolded.'

Meanwhile, back at Souljawn Records, John Ansdell had big plans for his first signing but they were somewhat limited by Emeli's continuing commitment to her degree. 'At the time she was in the middle of studying to be a doctor and I think her view was that she should really finish her degree first and then see what happens with music,' he says. 'The priority at the time was definitely her degree and at that time she was still a few years away from completing it. Because of the talent that she had, I thought she could have pushed it more but she's a very intelligent person and at the time it probably was a smarter move. I said to her, "If nothing else, just let the local community know what you're about and that's what I sold to her."'

So a plan was devised to release a short album giving a flavour of Sandé's music and have it ready in time for a showcase gig in December at the Òran Mór venue in Glasgow, a favourite hangout of Emeli's. Time was tight if everything was to be ready on time. John Ansdell: 'We'd pop round to each other's places quite often and we came up with a plan with a timeline. I left the creative stuff up to her. She was a producer and she made music on her laptop, so I left it up to her to continue writing and picking her top songs so she could release them as an album. Through the university she had a friend called Luigi and they handled the whole recording process. I was responsible for the promotional side of things and my plan was always to have a big launch in Glasgow. I booked Òran Mór in the west end of Glasgow. Everything was geared towards that, doing posters, word of mouth.'

Ansdell's family were also brought in to help with Project Sandé. His sister Megan, a keen photographer, took photos of the singer and some can be seen in this book. His dad, an ex-journalist, interviewed Emeli and helped put together a press pack to publicise her work.

Flyers for the gig on 18 December 2007 show a smiling Sandé with a tumble of curls, gold beads and a pink-and-blue summer dress. SOULJAWN RECORDS PRESENTS ADELE SANDE, the advert states, omitting the accent at the end of her surname. Special guests are promised at the gig and the price to get in is £6. A quote from Radio 1Xtra's Ras Kwame's about Emeli being reminiscent of Ella Fitzgerald is also featured.

John Ansdell wanted the show to be a cut above the usual ones he'd seen. He didn't want to present Emeli on her own – he wanted a full show that would show off the singer to best effect. 'I'd been to see R&B acts and they'd have a backing track or DJ. Emeli was just better than that so I wanted it to be a full band. I sourced a group of session musicians. We had a drummer, bass player, percussionist, keyboard player. Emeli also played keyboards. We had a beat boxer and four backing vocalists. We went completely all out.

That ate up an awful lot of my small business loan and my grant!'

Not everything went quite according to plan in the run up to the big launch. The CDs of Emeli's eight-track album – now called *Have You Heard?* – only arrived in the nick of time and didn't include the song of the same name that was supposed to be the title track. Despite what the flyers promised, there was no support act either. 'We'd put posters all over the west end of Glasgow,' recalls John Ansdell. 'The doors opened at seven and by half past seven there was hardly anyone there. It was horrible. I didn't know how many people were going to turn up. I just wanted it to be a really good night. In the next hour hundreds of people came through the door – just short of five hundred people. A lot of people came down from Aberdeen – her parents were there. I brought a lot of people too: family, friends and work colleagues.'

Ansdell got DJ and long-term Sandé supporter David Craig to introduce her on the night. 'I can remember the night clearly,' Craig told me. 'It was a fantastic night. I think it was a Tuesday so I wasn't expecting much by way of people – but it was packed. There was a fantastic anticipation about the whole thing. She was bubbling under and people were really excited to see what she was going to bring to the show. That was the night when I saw her and she turned a corner and I thought, you're not that shy little girl any more. She looked believable that night. There were A&Rs from London there who'd flown up and I think there were people from Radio 1Xtra there too. They were all pretty taken by her. There was air of inevitability about where she was heading, but she was still studying at that stage. I remember she did a cover of Ol' Dirty Bastard's 'Got Your Money' (the super-sweary 1999 track from the late Wu-Tang Clan man that featured Kelis). I remember saying that she was the only person who could make that track sound soulful.'

Emeli later explained why she had included the ODB track in her set: 'My background in music is really eclectic so I love listening to hip hop, but I find it hard to bring it into my own music because I don't have a big beat behind me [when playing live], but I thought, why not?' she told the Soul Interviews website. 'So the ODB cover just had a few simple chords then I sang his rap, but when I do it with a band it brings something completely different. I love doing things like that – putting my own twist on it. I try and put some lady elements into it.'

One reason the Òran Mór event was so packed could be put down to a little bit of identity confusion as to who the headline act actually was. Two months earlier, a new artist had released her debut single 'Hometown Glory' and it had reached No 19 in the charts. It would not be the first time that Adele Sandé would be confused with Londoner Adele Adkins. The singer in question – who'd go on to have massive worldwide success with her albums *19* and *21* – is almost universally referred to among the Scottish contributors to this story as 'London Adele'. 'A couple of people said to me that they thought it was London Adele appearing at the Òran Mór show,' admits John Ansdell. 'That could have had something to do with it. But I think I knew 350 out of the 500 people there. We didn't have a support act. The band just went out and started playing and Emeli came out and just killed it. Incredible. She just ticked every box even back then. She had an amazing voice, really good songwriter, great pianist, she arranged and produced all the tracks herself – [she had] a different image back then but she really looked the part.'

David Craig: 'Speaking to her afterwards the degree was still the important part and the music could wait till afterwards. I was really struck by her confidence and her faith that everything would happen at the right time.'

Around this time, Craig did an interview with Emeli for the Soul Interviews website. In it she outlined her hopes for her career – they were remarkably accurate in terms of how things would eventually work out. 'It would just be amazing to have a lot of people knowing your songs and not having worry about only a few people turning up to your gigs it would just be fantastic to have your music out there,' she said. 'I always want to be individual and do my own thing but I can understand how you might be under some compromise to do that when you're just starting off, with people saying do this and this and that will open the door, but do you really want your first step to be something that isn't you? I just want to be in the position to do my own thing and have people around me who trust what I'm doing and have people waiting to see what I'm going to be doing next. Just to be in a position where I can release music and a lot of people will be there to listen to it.'

It's believed that between 100 and 150 copies of *Have You Heard?* were sold at the Òran Mór gig that night. If you have a copy, then I suggest you take good care of it. It's worth a few quid.

Imagine you'd been there that night. You'd seen the show, liked the young singer and decided to buy a copy of her CD on the way out. You put the disc into CD player in your car. What would you have heard?

There are eight tracks on *Have You Heard?* – there should have been nine but that pesky title track wasn't quite ready. Six of the tracks are fully produced, one is acoustic and one is from a show that Sandé did for the BBC.

First up is 'Best Friend', a song for Diane Sandé. At first glance, there appears to be little here: brushes, rim shots and tumbling jazz piano chords, the kind of fluttering, descending notes that rappers like to sample. When Sandé sings – often double-tracking and riffing with herself – it comes alive. Lyrically, we are on course for the kind of themes that Sandé fans who bought *Our Version of Events* will be familiar with: keep your focus, stay up, don't get down, keep your head above water and everything's going to be all right. The track is barely more than three minutes in length but it does what a great song should do: leaves you wanting more.

Next is 'Baby's Eyes' – written for her boyfriend Adam Gouraguine. 'When I started writing songs I always promised myself I'd never write a love song,' Sandé later told *The Independent Music Show* when asked about the song. 'That's what everyone does. But I got to 16 or 17 and I found a boy. So that was my first ever love song. I'm glad I didn't write it in a cheesy manner. It still means the same to me now.'

'Baby's Eyes' is a late-night jazz number – voice and piano, nothing more. It's not a million miles from the way Emeli sang it in John Ansdell's flat the first time they met – it exudes atmosphere. It's like it's being performed in an almost empty nightclub just before closing time. Sandé's voice invokes a range of other performers, from Alicia Keys to Ella Fitzgerald and even British jazz stalwart Cleo Laine. David Craig: 'I remember hearing that song and thinking, how does an 18-year-old kid write stuff like that? That could have sat on her album [*Our Version of Events*] or even on a second album.'

Track three is 'Has Needs' and it's Sandé with her sexy head on, plain and simple. Sliding, upright bass, electric piano and tiny vocal gasps usher in a simple tale of A Woman. Who has needs. And the man in question, who is taking her there. You get the idea. As if to mirror the subject matter, there are vocal gymnastics aplenty and those familiar with Sandé's later work – and her somewhat prim image – will be surprised by the track.

'Silent' is just Emeli and a piano and it sounds more like a work in progress than the finished article. A metaphorical riff on the right to remain silent during arrest, the song – more of a tonal poem in fact – it's barely two minutes long and is gone before the listener can work out what it's actually about.

'Dirty Jeans & Sweater' is a short track but a real curiosity in as much as it features Emeli beat boxing – it also features her voice multi-tracked – and is perhaps a good example of Sandé the producer. A real curio.

'Patchwork' is next, a straight-ahead, late-night piano ballad. It's unusual mainly for its peculiar lyrical theme: 'I wrote it in about half an hour,' she explained in a very early interview with David Craig. 'Each verse is about something ending. If you have a relationship ending – a relationship with anything, with a person or a drug or something you're obsessed with – it starts off great and sweet and really amazing and slowly you get more and more involved in the world. You don't take anything else into consideration and in the end they're in bed and there's a fire and they're dying.'

'Your Song' is another late-night and low-key piece, just a touch of electric piano and some strings towards the end. It has a 1970s feel and a hippyfied lyric. The final track is 'Woman's Touch', the live piece recorded at the BBC – a proper piece of Neo Soul with a righteous lyric and a Fender Rhodes retro piano sound.

In one of her first ever interviews – with Urban Scot's David Craig – Emeli explained what she was trying to achieve with her early sound. 'All I can really do is to bring something that's honest to me,' she said. 'I'm just trying to bring as many influences as possible. I don't want to go down an R&B route, I don't want to go down an electro route – I just want to bring everything together and bring it with a good performance and with a good voice. That's what I think I'm bringing and I think, especially in the UK with soul, it goes down one street without any variation and I just want to mix it up a bit.'

In the form that it appeared on the night of the

Òran Mór gig, the *Have You Heard?* album is now gone. After much soul-searching, John Ansdell signed the tracks over to Virgin. He believes they may appear in some form in the future – perhaps as an EP or as an add-on to a future Sandé release. Maybe they won't appear at all. It's possible the description above might be the closest you get to hearing *Have You Heard?* in its entirety. In terms of those involved, there are mixed opinions about its merits, but the man who put up the money to fund it has no regrets. 'Obviously I feel really proud of what I did with her,' John Ansdell says. 'I will never claim to have discovered her or be responsible for what she's done. I'm glad that I was part of the puzzle in the beginning.'

David Craig believes that despite its strengths, the album's timing just wasn't right. 'It was probably best for her that she didn't get the thing with John released at the time,' Craig told me. 'I'm not sure she was ready. She wasn't the complete package then, though she was an amazing prospect and she ticked every single box. There are still great tracks on there that would have sat nicely on her album. If John put them out it would detract from the things she's done.'

Urban Scot's Mel Awasi thinks that Emeli could have made it around this time if she'd chosen to – she simply chose not to. 'It could have happened before if she'd wanted it to happen,' he told me. 'She was a talented artist before anyone came on the scene.

Everyone who met and worked with her, they all contributed and helped spread the word about her, but it was only a matter of time before she was going to make it.'

What about Sandé herself? How does she now view *Have You Heard?* 'God, that just feels so long ago,' she told Scotland's *Herald* newspaper in 2012. 'I feel like I've really progressed, and my writing's got better, and my understanding of pop music, and melody, has just improved so much since then. When I look back at the different types of music I've made since I was young, it's just who I'm listening to, and different inspirations. I think when a lot of songs were written for that first EP, I was listening to a lot of neo soul – Lauryn Hill and everyone.'

It seems a shame that nothing from *Have You Heard?* made it onto what most people assume to be Emeli's debut album, *Our Version of Events*. 'Baby's Eyes' in particular is a song that most hearers believe can stand alongside any of her later work. It's almost as if the 'old Emeli' had to be put to one side, to allow the 'new Emeli' to come through.

But back to Glasgow, December 2007. The Òran Mór launch was a success – far more successful than the slightly chaotic run-up to the gig might have suggested – and the next moves were already being planned. Emeli was going back up north for Christmas and was due to return to university at the end of January. A cut-down, digital version of the *Have You Heard?* album was set to be released in the New Year, with more to follow. John Ansdell: 'I was on quite a high after the gig and wanted to make the most of the opportunities. After the gig I had a couple of grand left and the plan was for Emeli to continue writing and recording tracks and to release a follow-up full album in 2008.'

Emeli did indeed record a follow-up album to *Have You Heard?* – but it wasn't released in 2008 and it wasn't on John Ansdell's Souljawn Records. It was on Virgin and it was called *Our Version of Events...* and it would turn Emeli Sandé into an international star.

Four

Her Name is Rio

At this time the singer at the heart of our story was going by her given name: Adele Sandé. The rise of 'London Adele' – Adele Adkins – seemed to cause a ripple of uncertainty in 'Scottish Adele'. Maybe it wasn't such a good idea to use her real name if she was going to try to make it as a singer? 'Adele had just received the Brits Critics' Award,' she told Q the Music. 'And I thought, oh, who's this girl? She's got my name! She's going to be big – I didn't think she was going to be this big.'

Urban Scot's Mel Awasi on Emeli: 'In 2008, we went to see her and she was thinking about changing her name, because of the other Adele. She was coming up with all sorts of different names and options.'

John Ansdell, the man behind the *Have You Heard?* album, says it showed how far Emeli believed she could go that she was worried about the similarity with 'London Adele'. 'It was shortly after the Òran Mór launch that "London Adele" took off and started to make an impression. Emeli said she didn't want any confusion. I thought it was funny at the time. My first instinct was, it's your name – why change it? It was great that even then she obviously had the ambition. She believed she could get to that level. We had so many chats about what she was going to call herself.'

It was clearly playing on her mind. One of her ideas – albeit a short lived one – would be to call herself Rio Sandé; she even went as far as to set up a MySpace account and played at least one gig under that name. She posted her thoughts on her existing 'listen2adele' MySpace page: 'OK so I've been thinking and thinking about this name issue and I thought... well, if I get to chose my own name, I should have a bit of fun with it!!' she wrote. 'So ladies and gentlemen... I introduce Rio Sandé!! Yep that's it! That's the one! Yes I know it sounds a little... funny, but let it sink in, live with it for a few days... go check out the page www.myspace.com/rioSandé add me!! I'll be putting any new music up there cos I'm gonna be slowly phasing this page out! OK... well this is going to be my pilot month, see how it fits!' Emeli signed off the blog: 'Rio... formerly known as Adele x.'

While Emeli wrestled with her identity crisis, John Ansdell was feeling like he could take on the world after the success of the Òran Mór album launch. He still had a little money left over and decided to look at recruiting more artists to his label. He looked at working with two-time *X Factor* contestant Chenai Zinyuku from Bradford, as well as Scottish rapper Kobi Onyami and Welsh singer songwriter Me One. By his own admission, Ansdell was spreading himself and the funds he had a bit thin. 'I guess I could have used a business advisor back then,' he says now. 'While all these things are happening, me and Emeli were still in touch and we met up and she played me some of her new songs which sounded amazing. I arranged a few more gigs in local venues; it came to the summertime when we should have been getting ready to release some more tracks and I had to have a horrible conversation with her. I was out of money. I'd already taken another loan out. I couldn't borrow any more. My parents gave me what they had. The way it was left was that I was going to go out and get investment so we could do this properly.'

Emeli didn't stand still, though, while this was going on. Around this time she blogged on her MySpace page that she was working with more Glasgow musicians, this time for local label Starla Records. Her deal with Souljawn was non-exclusive so she was free to work with anyone she pleased. Sandé's role was to be a guest vocalist. 'Up here in G town I'm working with some great musicians on Starla Records,' she wrote. 'We have penned a really great track called "Moving" – it has a real authentic Motown vibe. I'm recording that next week and can't wait for you all to hear it!!'

Starla was a recently formed 'boutique' label, started by friends Marco Rea, Craig Reece and Mark Robb. 'We were always on the look out for new acts and new singers,' Robb told me. 'Starla is a vinyl, 45 label. We do 500 copies every few months – it's a labour of love, but a good springboard for new bands and new soul and funk – and we sell them to DJs and connoisseurs throughout the world. The way we operate is very much through friends of friends. We were told about this girl who was a fantastic singer – people told us, you should get her in.'

The DT6 – Starla's 'house band' – had a tune called '(Theme From) The Baden Persuader', a Hammond organ and brass-driven instrumental that sounded like the soundtrack to a lost TV spy series from the 1960s. They needed a singer for a second track to make up the double A-side release they were planning. 'Marco had this song and Emeli came along to the studio,' Mark Robb explained to me. 'We'd been told she had an amazing voice and she certainly had, and she ended up recording on the session. At that time she'd been working with some guys down south but nothing had really broke for her, nothing compared to her being catapulted into the stratosphere like she was about to be. From my experience she was a lovely person. I believe she was a student at Glasgow University at the time. When I saw her later I couldn't believe the transformation in terms of her physical appearance. Back then she was a quietly spoken, polite, affable young lady who came up to the studio and did the work. What was refreshing for me at the time was that it was lovely working with someone with no ego, a great attitude, an intelligent person who broke though – my God she broke through – and hopefully she's retained those values. You're so used to working with people who'll step on anyone on the way up – she was very much the opposite of that.'

The track that Emeli appeared on alongside Marco Rea and The DT6 was eventually called 'Takes' and turned out to be a faux Northern Soul piece, with staccato drums, busy bass, a psychedelic middle-eight and a raft of clarinets across the top. It's a rather 'everything including the kitchen sink affair' and sounds like the kind of Mod/soul revival single that was common in the early 1980s. It's Sandé, but not as we know her.

The Starla team said goodbye to Emeli and wished her all the best for the future. The next time they saw her she looked and sounded very different. 'It's not that we didn't recognise her talent,' says Mark Robb.

'Maybe we should have worked more with her – but at that stage she did us a favour. She was like, you're local guys, I like the music. Let's do it. But she was on the verge of something in London. So it wasn't a case of working with Starla Records is going to push me on – she was already getting there.'

Meanwhile, Emeli's search for her musical identity was continuing. It was at the same time as she was involved with Starla that she flirtted with the idea of using the name Rio. Starla Records' Mark Robb has a music venue in Partick that regularly plays host to singers and musicians on the Glasgow scene. The name of the venue is the Rio Cafe. 'No way!' says Robb when I told him about the connection. Is that where the inspiration came from?

Emeli couldn't seem to make up her mind about her name. 'She decided to go with Rio and she did a couple of gigs and even set up a MySpace page as Rio Sandé,' confirms John Ansdell. 'But the feedback was that people thought it was Rio Grande and it didn't quite work out.'

Urban Scot's Mel Awasi: 'People were coming up with ideas. That's when she came up with the idea of using Emeli. She sent feelers out to all sorts of people asking, what do you think?'

'She talked to family and friends,' recalls John Ansdell. 'I pushed for Emeli because it had the different spelling, which made it unique.'

Emeli later told Qtv how she finally arrived at the decision: 'I really thought that if I'm going to distinguish myself as my own artist then I need my own name, and Emeli's my middle name so I picked that.'

The release of the Starla Records' double A-side of '(Theme From) The Baden Persuader' and 'Takes' was released just in time for it to feature her 'new' name: Emeli Sandé. Not only that, it got Emeli what must have been her first review from the Monkeyboxing funk and soul website. Sadly, it was not a great one: 'Starla do their double A side 45 thing again and once more I find myself loving one track and running in fear from the other,' the reviewer said. 'I googled "The Baden Persuader" (the one I like) intrigued by the "Theme from" prefix, expecting to find links telling me about some sort of German *Get Carter*-style movie. All I got were references to this very track though, which, as it turns out, finds Starla house band The DT6 dropping eastern-sounding instrumental spy-flick funk so sinuous you could put a leather jacket on it and call it a snake. Flipside "Takes", in contrast, comes across as an 80s update on 60s northern soul and for all the fact that Emeli Sandé and Marco supply quality vocals, it's got Costa Del Crime 80s mirror ball disco written all over it. Shiny and evil.'

Alongside changing her name, studying for her degree, releasing an indie album and being a guest star for Starla Records, Emeli also found time to play shows in Madrid and in her boyfriend Adam Gouraguine's native Montenegro. 'I've done a few shows in Montenegro and he's been my translator,' she told the *Daily Record*. 'I wouldn't expect my music to be appreciated over there but they just love jazz and there's such a crowd for that sort of thing. I couldn't speak their language but I can communicate through music. It was really cool. Adam is a marine biologist but he appreciates music and loves listening to my stuff and if I've written a little song I'll always show him first. But he's not musical – I've tried to teach him piano a few times but he got really impatient. I had to leave that one.'

Meanwhile Emeli was continuing with her networking in and around the music industry and on both sides of the border. One meeting around this time would have a major impact on her fortunes and her future. She was becoming a regular at showcase events for up-and-coming talent, mainly in London. One of these showcases was for Radio 1Xtra, the younger, more urban sister station to Radio 1. Emeli's mum Diane would send CDs of her work to the recently launched station, even getting some airplay from DJ Ras Kwame. There was no compromise to the format of Kwame's shows and he would play Sandé's music – just her at a piano – in between his more usual, harder playlist.

It was at one of these 1Xtra events in Soho in London that she met Shahid Khan, otherwise known as Naughty Boy. 'It was the end of 2008 and she opened the show and I was just amazed,' Khan later told *Sound on Sound* magazine. 'I didn't know who she was and I couldn't believe everyone else in the room wasn't reacting like me. Afterwards I just went up and spoke to her. She was just there with her sister and she was going back to Scotland. We stayed in touch for a few weeks and she heard some of the music I'd done with Bashy (actor and musician Ashley Thomas) and she sent me over some stuff that she'd done.'

Khan was an up and coming producer who, like John Ansdell, had been a beneficiary of the Prince's Trust. He'd managed to get a £5,000 Trust grant and used it to set up a recording studio in his parents' garden shed in their home town of Watford. 'Basically, half the shed was my mum's pots and pans that she wouldn't be using and half was my studio,' he later said.

But the real financial kick to Khan's career came from an even more unlikely source than the Prince's Trust – it came from Noel Edmonds. Khan had entered the Channel 4 show *Deal or No Deal*, and managed to win £44,000. '*Deal or No Deal* was 2006. It was the start of the journey,' Naughty Boy told journalist John Dingwall. 'I dropped out of a degree course and I did two things. I applied to The Prince's Trust and *Deal or*

No Deal. I had thought one of them would work because I needed a laptop and some software to be taken seriously. I got both. That was the start. I wasn't nervous on *Deal or No Deal* because they had kept me there for 26 shows. I was opening boxes first for other contestants. Because I was there for a month, by the time I was playing I was so ready that I wasn't nervous.' According to the budding producer he became quite a cult figure on the show: 'I even had a Shahid Khan fan club on the *Deal or No Deal* forum. I dealt and I beat the banker. In my box, I had £35,000 and I dealt at £44,000. I'm in the *Deal or No Deal* game as a character and they asked me to be in the Comic Relief sketch with Catherine Tate.'

He ploughed the cash into upgrading his shed-cum-studio and setting up his own record label. By the time he met Sandé in 2008, he was itching for the big break. 'We got in the studio and we clicked workwise,' Emeli later explained to journalist Cara Sulieman. 'I just really enjoyed listening to what he was doing – it was so different from other people's stuff.' Shahid Khan: 'She started flying down every other week and she'd stay in a bed and breakfast just round the corner and we'd write together. That's when it really kicked off.'

The contrast between the studious Sandé and the streetwise Khan couldn't have been greater – but that seems to have been the basis and reason for the success of their relationship. 'We were from very different backgrounds,' Khan told the *London Evening Standard* in 2013. 'She was going to be a doctor and I was a marketing and music dropout at London Guildhall, delivering pizzas for Domino's. She made me take myself a lot more seriously. The way I approached making music changed dramatically when I started working with her.'

It turned into a time of intense hard work and creativity for Sandé, not least because she was slap bang in the middle of her degree at the time. 'Her work ethic was remarkable,' Adrian Sykes, the man who is now her manager, later recalled in an interview with the *Daily Record*. 'Monday to Thursday, she would be walking the wards and attending lectures and doing what young trainee doctors do. Then she would fly down to London on Thursday night and be in the studio until Sunday night. She'd fly back up to Glasgow on Monday morning, get on a white coat, put the stethoscope around her neck and start all over again. She worked incredibly hard.'

'We just started writing, not necessarily for me,' recalls Sandé about her working partnership with Khan. 'We just thought, let's write a pop tune and experiment.'

The pop tune they wrote began a series of events that would make Emeli one of the biggest music stars in the world.

Five

Let the Writing Commence

The first pop tune that Emeli and Naughty Boy wrote became 'Diamond Rings' after Khan sent it to Vash Sia Khatiri, the manager of young London rapper Jahmaal Noel Fyffe, better known as Chipmunk. He was in the market for material and collaborators for his upcoming album.

The song began life as a sample from a record Khan had found in a charity shop – 'Miss Ska-Culation' by saxophonist Roland Alphonso, a 1960s ska cover version of 'Pipeline' by US surf group The Chantays. 'I used to buy CDs from Oxfam of old ska tunes,' Khan later explained to journalist Matt Frost. 'I didn't know what I was buying really, but I just heard that sample [from 'Miss Ska-Culation'] and I heard the beat around it and I just took a chance, really. UK rappers were underground then, and that was Chipmunk's first commercial hit, and I was really into how to bridge that gap between still rapping and still being British but making it on Radio 1. I always thought that ska had that sound and reggae in general had that sound where you could rap on it. It could still be quite commercial but would still be cool. I wanted to use a sample which embodied all that, and that track did. I just built some drums around it and it was one of the first things me and Emeli did together as well. I think Emeli wrote that hook while she was hoovering!'

Chipmunk shared the songwriting credit with Emeli and Naughty Boy for the track and Sandé's voice was kept on the finished piece. But not everyone was convinced that the 'Diamond Rings' track showed Emeli in the best possible light. John Ansdell: 'I remember she came round to my flat and she got a phone call from Chipmunk. He played the "Diamond Rings" track down the phone to her and she put it on speakerphone and we had a listen to it. I hadn't heard of Chipmunk at the time. I had to look him up. I didn't think it did her any justice. He seemed quite established so it was going to be good exposure for her, so in that sense I thought it was great.'

Even Sandé's dad Joel wasn't entirely convinced to start with: '"Diamond Rings" is a very catchy song but when she first sent it up to us to listen to, we thought it was a bit odd,' he told Scottish website Deadline News. 'It grows on you – I think everyone thinks that about it.'

Whatever the merits of the track, it served a definite purpose as far as Emeli was concerned – she was in the business of learning her craft. 'Working for other people was a great learning curve for me, because it really made me understand the music industry,' she later told the AllHipHop website. 'It made me understand radio. It also made me see that when working with different artists and just seeing how different teams work, unless you specifically know what you want to say, other people are going to decide for you. That, for me, was like, before I even attempt to be an artist, I need to know exactly what I want to say and what type of artist I want to be.'

Eventually released in July 2009, 'Diamond Rings' would become a No 6 hit for Chipmunk in the UK. 'It's just strange that some little song that I wrote in my bedroom has had so much success and airplay,' Sandé said at the time. 'It's crazy.' Her vocals were probably the best thing about the lightly skanking track, but Emeli didn't appear in the video because of the pressure of work from her degree course. 'I was so determined to finish so I went back and I tried to put everything that had happened to the back of my mind,' she said. Her part is taken by an actress who lip-synchs along to the gangster-themed promo, which actually looks more *Bugsy Malone* than *Scarface*.

Emeli was able to be at Chipmunk's side at the SECC in Glasgow in October. The track had been nominated for a Music of Black Origin (MOBO) award as best song. She appeared – her trademark curls bigger than ever – alongside Chipmunk and a troupe of dancers at the show. The nomination and the SECC appearance were key moments for Sandé – her first taste of a massive audience in a huge venue. Her profile was rising in the Scottish media and her parents Joel and Diane were collared by journalists backstage. 'It doesn't matter if she wins or not. Performing at the MOBOs is the most exciting part of the experience – if "Diamond Rings" wins the award then that would be the icing on the cake.' Dad Joel added: 'It is good that she is getting recognition now after all the work she has put in. We used to sit and watch other people getting signed up and performing and I would think, my Adele [Emeli] is better than them. And now everyone has noticed how good she is.'

It would be a good night for Chipmunk – he won Best Single and Best Hip Hop Act at the MOBOs. Though he shared the first award with Sandé, her success has very much eclipsed his over the intervening years. But the Chipmunk connection would prove to be a vital one for both Emeli and Naughty Boy. As a result of Chipmunk's interest in the track, music publisher Danny D – the man who accompanied Sykes to Alford to see Sandé when she was 16 – gave her a publishing deal, signing her to Stellar Songs at EMI.

The fact that a Glasgow student had managed to get a publishing deal and a song into the charts while still at university generated a little early publicity for Emeli and she was interviewed alongside her parents by Deadline News: 'I am now a professional songwriter,' she said. 'I have been working to this since I was 11. Eleven years later here I am – let the writing commence.'

Her parents, though, were clearly a little more cautious about the whole thing. Education very clearly came first as far as the Sandés were concerned. 'She has worked very hard for the last few years to get here,' said her mum Diane. 'Not only does she put all the effort into her music, but she manages to juggle it with her studies as well. We're very pleased that she has decided to keep on at her studies – her degree is very important to us as a family. But equally I said to her when she left to go to university that she needed to make time for her music. Writing and performing is a passion for her and I think it's helpful for her to have these two very different things in her life. They balance each other out. She's said that she's met a lot of other people on her course who have very creative hobbies so it must be a common combination.'

Naughty Boy also got a deal with Sony/ATV and the money allowed him to move his studio out of his parents' shed and into a space at Ealing Studios. Khan dubbed the new studio Cabana and the first song he and Sandé wrote in it was 'Heaven' – the track that would become Sandé's debut solo hit.

'Diamond Rings' also signalled the start of a series of tracks written for a wide variety of other artists under the Khan/Sandé imprint, both as a duo and as part of other songwriting teams. They managed to get a B side hit in the charts in the shape of 'Boys' for Cheryl Cole – the subject matter of romantically open girls being wary of bad boys must have chimed with the former Girls Aloud singer and TV talent show judge. Cole's version is remarkably similar to Sandé's demo, but its sing-the-verse-on-a-single-note style suited Cole's voice better. Emeli and Khan didn't collaborate directly with Cole on the song – an indication of their growing positions of songwriters to order. 'That was kind of like an email job,' Sandé later said when asked how the 'collaboration' came about by MTV. 'Her A&R was in control of what she was doing and had heard that we write and wanted something from us. We had written a song that was quite pop and we thought it might suit her, so it kind of happened like that.' The song was the back-up track on the single '3 Words', a No 4 hit for Cole in December 2009.

'Seeing other people sing my work is great,' Emeli

told the AllHipHop website, 'because the way I write is an emotional way of writing, and I'm always very honest – no matter if the song is for me or for somebody else. So, when I see people interpret what I'm singing, they're usually interpreting it in a way that's emotional for them. They're never faking it, so I love seeing different people's interpretations. They found something in their life or their emotions that is connected with that song. It's always interesting for me to see that.'

The next Sandé/Naughty Boy release – 'Radio' for TV pundit and former Mis-Teeq singer Alesha Dixon – was an A side but only made it to No 46 in the UK charts. Despite its big chorus, the song was perhaps too slow for radio itself and may have been hampered by an over-edgy, domestic abuse themed video. But another key breakthrough was 'Let Go' which appeared on rapper Tinie Tempah's debut album *Disc-Overy*. Released in October 2009, the album made it to No 1 and was nominated for a Mercury Music Prize. 'Let Go' propped up the end of the album and features a distorted vocal from Sandé, a sweary rap from Tempah (who ironically raps that none of his songs are written for him by other people) and a typically stripped-back production from Naughty Boy. 'I really feel part of a big wave that's happening in British music at the moment and that's really exciting,' Emeli told Scottish journalist Nicola Meighan. 'I've been so lucky to work with Naughty Boy, Chipmunk and Tinie – being on the UK's No 1 album was incredible! There's like a mutual respect, and it feels like a community. And with me coming from Scotland, it's so nice that I can be involved in it and be part of it.'

Despite the obvious creative productivity in her songwriting, some people around her were surprised that Emeli didn't want to get her own voice out there centre stage. DJ David Craig: 'I remember saying to her, "Are you not getting frustrated? Surely you want to get your own stuff out?" She didn't seem to be in any rush. I never, ever got any sense that she doubted herself. Though she was very shy initially, I wouldn't be surprised if she never doubted herself for a minute.'

Sandé wanted to keep some of the songs that were coming through to herself – the main prize was still a record deal and an album of her own. 'There were a few that I'd definitely had to fight to keep for myself,' she later told the BBC, 'because when you're a writer and everyone is coming to you for music, it's so tempting if someone says, "We'll give you a cheque for whatever you want for this song." But it means something to you and you know that if I'm successful as an artist I want this on my album. So there are songs like "Clown" and "Mountains" that I really fought quite hard to keep.'

Despite the groundswell of interest in Sandé and her music, she was still insisting that her education came first and that she could juggle both with the help of her parents and manager Adrian Sykes. 'Adrian really respects that I want to get an education behind me,' she told the *Daily Record* in July 2009. 'He also knows my parents are keen that I finish university. It's really good having people behind you who aren't rushing you to do something or respect what you're trying to achieve. I've managed to pass my exams in medicine and make things happen in music, so the plan is to continue to try and balance it for the next two years and I'll see how that goes.'

In September 2009, Emeli began the fourth year of her degree in Glasgow. She'd had a summer holiday like few students could imagine. She'd notched up a hit record, got a publishing deal and become a professional songwriter. 'Back in lectures,' she posted on her Facebook site. 'Did this summer really happen??'

But soon the conflict between her music and her education finally came to a head. The unexpected success of placing 'Diamond Rings' with Chipmunk meant that, in the words of manager Adrian Sykes, 'Things snowballed much quicker than we had anticipated. With that exposure we decided to make a plan; 18 months was going to be the time where we wanted to get things cracking. By then we were fully in the mould. It was something that we sensed. So she went to have a serious talk with her parents about her new plans.'

The reaction she got – particularly from someone who held education in such importance as Joel Sandé – wasn't what she was expecting. 'My decision to go to university had been my own,' she later told journalist Matt Munday. 'It wasn't anything my dad had enforced. But when I rang Dad and told him I was thinking of putting my medical studies on hold, I was surprised that he was totally fine about it. He just said, "You know what? If this is what you want to do, you may as well give it 100 per cent." Knowing he was behind me when I made that decision was really important to me. I hope I never let him down.'

Emeli took a week out of her studies and went to America. That's when the final decision was made. 'I went to New York for a week and was meeting musicians and everything and thought, I really want this,' she later said. 'So that's when I left.'

Glasgow University clearly didn't hold her early exit against her – Emeli was named Young Alumnus of the Year in 2011. 'The Young Alumnus title is an important one for Glasgow,' Professor Anton Muscatelli, the principal and vice-chancellor of the University of Glasgow, said in a press statement released at the time of the award. 'It is a chance for us to recognise the achievements of former students who have made a major contribution to the community, arts, science or business. Emeli joins a distinguished group of previous winners including Professor Patrick

Gunning for his work on more effective and less toxic cures for cancer and Scotland international rugby player, Euan Murray. Emeli is an extremely talented young woman ... She will be an excellent ambassador for the University of Glasgow.'

Emeli's ties with the university continued – in June 2013 she was awarded an honorary degree to mark her musical rather than medical skills. Professor John Briggs, vice-principal of the University, said: 'The University of Glasgow is very pleased to recognise Emeli Sandé's huge contribution to music, both in the UK and around the world, by awarding her an honorary degree. It's also a privilege to be able to honour eight other figures who are recognised as leaders both within their own fields of expertise, and beyond.'

Looking back, Sandé has since said that her medical studies made her less 'desperate' than many musicians – she had another, considerable string to her bow if things didn't work out. She later told Clare Balding on Radio 2: 'It wasn't a case of I'd do anything to be signed. It was a lot more on my terms. I loved medicine. It wasn't a case of settling for medicine. I just thought, this will be a nice life and it's secure and I don't have to risk moving to London and pursuing a dream. So there was definitely moments where I thought, you know what, I want to be a psychiatrist or a neurologist, but there was just something inside of me. I would see people who were just so passionate about medicine; they would spend all day speaking about medicine. I loved medicine. But I felt that way about music. So at that point I thought, I need to do this.'

Urban Scot's Mel Awasi has his own theory about why Sandé changed her mind. 'I think her mum and dad kept her focus on her studies. Maybe it got to the stage where her parents realised there were opportunities coming at her from all directions. I think her parents must have kind of given up! Let's just do it, let's just go for it.'

But the main prize was still a record deal. Sandé even auditioned for Take That star Gary Barlow, who'd just set up a new label called Future Records. The future judge on *The X Factor* – who would have a degree of label success with classical singer Camilla Kerslake and rapper Aggro Santos – wasn't convinced when Sandé went to audition for him and sang a song that would turn out to be a stand-out track on *Our Version of Events*. 'I watched as she sang "Clown",' Naughty Boy later said in a 2013 interview with the *Daily Record*. 'He listened and said that he didn't think she was a star. Emeli's performance was identical to how she performed the song at *The X Factor* final. It's crazy. On *The X Factor* he is a judge of potential stars and yet he couldn't even spot the biggest star in the country right now. I find that a bit disheartening ...

Emeli could have lost confidence when Gary Barlow told her she wouldn't be a star ... it could have knocked Emeli's confidence and she could have walked away from music. There was other label interest and a lot was happening, but we didn't know where we stood. Imagine if Virgin hadn't come along and signed her.' Barlow's rejection of Sandé at that audition may well have been the best thing happened to her. Future Records went out of business in 2012, just as Emeli has achieving her greatest successes.

There were clearly no hard feelings on Emeli's part though – she would write a track called 'Find a Boy' that was recorded by one of Barlow's signings, singer A*M*E. What's more, when in 2013 Sandé performed 'Clown' in *The X Factor* final, with Gary Barlow on the judging panel, he stood up and applauded when Emeli had finished.

As Emeli still searched for that elusive record deal, there was talk of her releasing an independent single – one song 'Daddy' was mentioned as a possible contender – but it was decided to take the well-trodden route of teaming her with an established, credible artist. She was paired with the Godfather of Grime, Wiley, otherwise known as rapper and MC Richard Kylea Cowie. The single was called 'Never Be Your Woman' – based around the 1997 UK No 1 'Your Woman' by White Town. 'I had always wanted to sample the White Town song and to hear what it would sound like with a woman's vocal since I was a kid,' said Naughty Boy, Emeli's collaborator on the song, in an interview with the *Daily Record*. 'One day I tried it with Emeli, who hadn't heard the song before, and she made it her own.'

'Never Be Your Woman' made Sandé's collaboration with Chipmunk seem very tame in comparison. Not only did she get a 'featuring' credit, she is also seen on screen, singing the chorus from a rooftop, still sporting her tumbling, curly hair. For some people who'd worked with her in the past, it was a surprise to see Emeli on TV in a music video: 'There was a video of her on an estate and I thought, that's that really nice girl who was singing for us,' Starla Records' Mark Robb recalls. 'But who could ever have determined how successful she was going to be?'

Though Wiley felt from the start that Emeli's talent was 'sky-high', he believed she wasn't mainstream enough to make it in Britain. 'I never thought Emeli would be a star in the UK. I thought she'd have to make it big in the US first,' he told the *Daily Star*. 'Ten years ago you'd never have had someone as unusual as Emeli winning *The X Factor*, so I thought she'd struggle as she's aimed at a similar market. But the star-making system has changed, and that's all good.'

The Wiley single – a No 8 hit in March 2010 and produced by Naughty Boy – became the catalyst for Sandé being offered a record deal by Virgin. 'I think by that point people had begun to realise what potential she had,' Sykes later told hitquarters.com. 'They heard more of Emeli's music and became more and more interested in what she was doing. Also, what with the great reviews she'd already had through the songwriting features, they were really excited about the possibilities of what they could do with her. It's all about being a visionary. Virgin saw the potential and took the risk.'

Meanwhile, while all this was going on, John Ansdell had been running around trying the raise the finance for Emeli's follow-up release on Souljawn records. He was trying increasingly exotic ways of raising the money he needed: 'I had a Wurlitzer piano which I sold but getting 500 quid here and there wasn't enough.' So John joined an entrepreneurial 'speed dating' service, meeting a series of wealthy potential investors who might be willing to put money into Emeli's next release. 'I had a lot of interest, but no one was willing to take a punt on me and Emeli. I had no contacts and no business background and she was still pretty much an unknown. It was too big a risk for them.'

Finally, John managed to find a single private investor willing to put up the money for a second Sandé album and he rushed to tell Emeli the news. She had some news of her own. 'I called up Emeli and said, "At last I've done it!" It was a lot of money in comparison to what we had before. It was more than enough. I knew it was enough to do her justice.'

Emeli told John that she had been offered a record deal. 'She had an offer on the table from Virgin,' Ansdell told me. 'I remember I called her on a Monday or Tuesday and she said she had to decide by Friday about the Virgin offer. I felt I never helped her reach her potential. I thought I could follow through with it but I couldn't compete with a major label. I said, "You should go with the Virgin offer." She's so talented I thought she deserved to have the proper backing.'

It transpired that the reason that many labels had turned her down was that her reputation as a songwriter had overshadowed her singing talent. 'The record labels saw me as a songwriter,' she later explained in an interview with the *Daily Record*. 'It was hard to get people to believe in me as an artist. I tried to bang down a lot of doors but Virgin were the only label who believed in what I was doing. I ended up with the label that understood what I was trying to do.'

Emeli signed to Virgin – John Ansdell had lost out. To this day, he is remarkably philosophical about the whole affair. 'We signed a non-exclusive contract,' he says today. 'If it had been exclusive – and I had handled the money I had better – I would have received something. But it was non-exclusive. So I didn't. I still genuinely don't feel bad about it. I'm happy she's got to where she is.'

'It was a long journey to get signed,' Emeli told journalist Simon Parkin. 'Once you get established as a songwriter it's quite hard to get people to recognise you as an artist in your own right. It felt like a long battle to get people to see me and believe in my music. Lots of labels didn't want to sign me. So it was great to prove people wrong in that sense.'

Despite losing out on Emeli's success, John Ansdell remained optimistic about his chances of signing the next big thing and continued to search for new talent. Surely, his luck would change? 'I was meeting new people and artists and making contacts,' he told me. 'One of the artists I was in touch with I contacted through MySpace. At the time she was unsigned. She had four or five demos on her MySpace page and she'd passed a million hits. I got in touch with this singer and said, 'This isn't my normal kind of music," but I proposed we release an EP together. She said, "Yeah, that sounds amazing." It looked like I was going to get her, then a major label came in and signed her. It was Paloma Faith.'

Six

A Massive Attack on the Charts

'I'm now an official recording artist with Virgin Records!! Let's go!!' is how Emeli posted the news of her record contract on her Facebook site. Her management – who'd waited patiently since she was a teenager to begin really guiding her career – now had a relatively simple plan when it came to launching her on the public: let people hear how good a singer she was, make them aware of her songwriting skills and then use those elements to build a following. 'One thing I wanted to make sure is that people realise that she is a real artist,' manager Adrian Sykes told music industry website hitquarters. 'She not only sings but she's an incredibly gifted songwriter, and she works really hard. She is a fairly old-fashioned artist in the sense that what you see and hear really is her. You get some artists now that sound great on radio but can't translate that live. Or they are an amazing live act but just can't get it right on record. Emeli, on the other hand, truly is a 360 degree artist.'

In June 2011 Emeli played at the RockNess music festival at Dores near Inverness in the Highlands of Scotland. The gig was touted as being the launch of her solo career. 'I'm excited about introducing myself this way,' she told the *Daily Record*, the Scottish tabloid newspaper that was starting to take a real interest in her career. 'It is quite daunting not to be the featured act, but it's exciting. I am really looking forward to the atmosphere at RockNess. I'm very excited because it is in Scotland. All my friends and family are going to come along.'

Emeli played on the Saturday of the three-day festival – The Chemical Brothers were top of the bill that day, and Emeli was well down the bill alongside the likes of Dog Is Dead and Bigfoot's Tea Party. Hard to believe now, but she still appeared to be hedging her bets as to whether she would return to university in the autumn. 'I realise I am probably not going to be a doctor now, but I enjoyed studying medicine. I did three years of pre-clinical medicine and did neuroscience for my fourth year because neurology is the most fascinating part of the course. I need to make a decision whether to go back soon, but I don't think I could walk away from music at the moment.'

Two days after the RockNess appearance, on 13 June, Emeli took a big step up the pecking order – and achieved an enormous personal ambition – as the opening act at London's Royal Albert Hall for Alicia Keys. The American singer, who had so inspired Emeli at the SECC in Glasgow when she was in her teens, was doing a stripped-down show at the London venue, just her and a piano. Reviewers fell over themselves to heap praise on the main act: 'Keys offered up a masterclass to her pop peers,' said the *Daily Telegraph*. 'A demonstration of how to match production pyrotechnics with the most elemental of musical tools – keyboard and voice, the art of the song.' The *Independent* said: 'She displays the prowess of a truly remarkable virtuoso, rarely missing a note during her generous two-hour performance.' The reviewers gave no space to the support act that night, but Emeli's time to shine at the Royal Albert Hall in her own right wouldn't be too long in coming.

Away from the live stage, more guest appearances were on the cards for Emeli's recorded output. They'd keep her name bubbling while she and Naughty Boy worked on her first album for Virgin. Her next feature spot was a canny one. With a shady past and a slim physique, Professor Green – otherwise known as Hackney rapper Stephen Manderson – had been touted as the English Eminem. By the spring of 2010 his blend of pop sensibility and street suss was paying dividends, with his INXS-sampling 'I Need You Tonight' single heading for the UK Top 3. A horrific nightclub attack in 2009 had left Green with a vicious scar across his neck, right through a tattoo that bore the legend 'lucky'. The grimly appropriate title of his debut album, released in July 2010, was *Alive Till I'm Dead*. The first track, 'Kids That Love to Dance', featured up-and-coming singer Emeli Sandé. Though it wasn't a single, a 'viral' video of the short, sharp, pop rap track was produced, inspired by the Chatroulette website where online link-ups are created at random. The track did the perfect job of not frightening new listeners who might be put off by the Professor's harder material. Green professed himself to be a major fan of his fellow Virgin artist. 'You don't often find people who are both profound and prolific,' he told Dropout UK. 'She's both of those, not to mention she can write and she can sing. And she's a nice girl on top of it, so you can't even hate her for all her talents!'

Sandé's urban credentials had been further increased by her association with Devlin. East London grime MC and rapper James Devlin was looking all set to be a breakout star with a series of mixtapes and EPs under his own name and collective banners along with the likes of future Sandé collaborator Wretch 32 and Scorcher. His debut album *Bud, Sweat and Beers* had been released in October 2010. As a trailer for the album, a single had been put out in August called 'Brainwashed', and Emeli received a co-writing credit with Devlin and Pontus Hjelm, a Swedish metal guitarist and EMI songwriter and producer. Quite a line-up. The end result – with a Sandé-esque vocal by London singer Milena Sanchez – had an epic feel, like the soundtrack to a crime movie that had yet to be made. It deserved to get higher in the charts than No 31, but it was still another Top 40 notch for Sandé as a songwriter. Two more tracks on Devlin's album would also have the Sandé touch: 'Yesterday's News' featured Naughty Boy among the writers but Emeli was credited as featured singer, adding a very low-key vocal line to the chorus of another widescreen Devlin rap. The third track involving Sandé was the best: 'Dreamer' starts with an Emeli vocal right from the start, a gentle skanking beat and a minimal backing for Devlin's rap. It wasn't a single – maybe it should have been. There's no doubt that Sandé's presence on the album lifted it several notches beyond the usual rap and brag affair.

By now, Emeli had moved to London – she really was 'London Adele'. 'It was the biggest risk I had ever taken because there was no guarantee that packing my stuff and moving to London would work out, but I knew that it was just something I felt really strongly about,' she told the *Hackney Gazette*. 'I was leaving a stable career and I'd worked very hard getting to medical school and all the rest of it, but I graduated at that point with a degree in neuroscience, so I felt that my years hadn't been wasted.'

The old 'Scottish Adele' was starting to fade away. Sandé's style had begun to change too and the Emeli Sandé we recognise today was starting to emerge. Tattoos began to be seen – eventually becoming quite a collection. 'Un Cuarto Propio' – Spanish for 'A Room of One's Own' would appear on her left forearm, a reference to an essay by author Virginia Woolf and a very direct declaration of independence. 'You do need your own place and your own money to create as good as the guys,' she told the *Daily Record*. On the right arm: the Mexican artist Frida Kahlo. 'Ring the bells of happiness!' she wrote on her blog. 'After 2 years of talking about it, thinking about it and chickening out... I finally did it! FRIDA KAHLO is finally on my arm!'

Kahlo's self-portraits, highlighting and celebrating her unconventional appearance, made her a feminist icon. 'Frida, I guess I saw her work in art class when I was in high school and then from then on, as I grew older as a woman, she meant more and more to me,' Sandé told Canada's QMI. 'I really understand how strong she had been as an artist. I feel like her portraits, in particular, the flaws are right there for you to see and it makes them so beautiful and strong. And as a woman within the [music] industry, there are certain kinds of rules and boxes people try and put you into. So seeing her reminds me to be a strong artist and to really compete with anybody whether they're a man or woman.'

On the back of her neck appeared the legend 'Did our last castle look like this?' 'The idea stemmed from a fascinating conversation I had about people you are certain you've loved and created with in a past life,' she later told the Voices on the Verge website. Her sister was celebrated with a 'First Lucy' tattoo on Emeli's wrist, and boyfriend Adam Gouraguine was also commemorated in ink, fittingly in his native Serbian – 'Volim to Adame' [I Love You Adam]. She even joked about immortalising another painter – Rolf Harris. 'A Rolf tattoo would certainly be an ice breaker at parties,' she claimed. 'I could get a really bad tattoo artist to do it, with the words: "Can you tell what it is yet?" written underneath.'

Then there was the hair. Her trademark tumble of afro curls would be replaced by an even more distinctive look. Within 18 months, Sandé's platinum buzz cut and quiff would be voted one of Britain's most iconic hairstyles, second only to the Duchess of Cambridge, Kate Middleton. It wasn't an overnight change. She wasn't bold enough to take such a radical leap in one go – the new Sandé look came gradually. 'I felt free and liberated,' she said about her move to London in an interview with Creative Head. 'It gradually got lighter and lighter and shorter and shorter and my hairdresser at the time said, "Baby gal, just do it already!" So we cut it all off and bleached it.' It wasn't actually the most radical haircut she'd ever had: 'My dad cut my hair when I was 10 and the result was two triangles on the side. My best friend still reminds me of it to this day.'

Adele from Alford in Aberdeenshire was gone. 'I felt it was a kind of rebellion,' she told journalist Teddy Jamieson about her changing style. 'Adele is the med student who was very sensible and quite studious. Emeli moved to London. Getting the hair and the tattoos, it definitely felt like an evolution into Emeli.'

For those who knew Emeli from Scotland, the changes in Sandé not only came from her developing independence – they suspected that it came from her record company too. 'Virgin made quite an effort to give her distinguishing features with the hair and everything,' John Ansdell believes today. 'Before she just dressed in normal clothes and she had a large afro. Jill Scott and Erykah Badu... similar kind of vibe.'

While this physical transformation was taking place, so was the take-up of Sandé's songs and lyrics by other artists – and they were contrasting to say the least. 'Let it Rain' was a Top 20 hit for Kwasi Danquah III – otherwise known as Tinchy Stryder – and featured vocals from Canadian R&B singer Melanie Fiona. 'This Will Be the Year' – a song by Sandé, Naughty Boy and Josh Kear, an American best known for country hits like 'Need You Now' by Lady Antebellum – was recorded as an album track by Susan Boyle for her 2011 release *Someone to Watch over Me*. The *Britain's Got Talent* runner-up had, under Simon Cowell's guidance, become a global phenomenon after defying the judging panel's expectations with her performance of 'I Dreamed a Dream' from *Les Miserables* on the show in 2009. The video of her audition had become a viral phenomenon. Since then she'd been given a sleek makeover and her first album had become the fastest selling UK debut in chart history. Boyle would later say that Emeli's song was her favourite track on *Someone to Watch over Me*.

'This Will Be the Year' was a regretful show song with a lyric about the seemingly forlorn hope of things getting better – just piano, strings and vocal. Sandé and Naughty Boy 'sold' the song when she was still a student and Emeli had described Boyle recording it as her 'proudest moment', something she later eased back from. 'We had just written a lot of songs and my background of writing is just by sitting at a piano and writing, so that's why I just love classic songs and they really liked it,' she later told MTV about how the collaboration came about. 'I don't know if it was my actual proudest moment, but it was quite cool. I haven't met her [Boyle] yet. I just sent her the song. I'd love to meet her because I think she is a bit of a rock star.'

When Sandé's success kicked in, many people raised their eyebrows that she had written for an avowedly middle-of-the-road singer like Boyle. 'I think she's got soul,' she later told The Quietus website. 'I'd seen a few documentaries and heard stories and she's very honest when she speaks. She's real. She has a lot more soul than a lot of people who call themselves soul singers. I just hear something in her voice and I knew that there was something in her that would relate to the way I write, and they told me that when she was recording my songs she was crying and I knew that she would find that connection. She needs music – and people who need music are the kind of people I want to write for.'

For a time it seemed like Sandé was in danger of becoming Simon Cowell's in-house writer: she was involved in three tracks for *X Factor* winner Leona Lewis. These included the single 'Trouble', which was cut from similar cloth to the track that would become Emeli's debut single, 'Heaven'. Another song initially earmarked for Lewis was reclaimed by Sandé with an eye on her own album: a song about her parents' relationship called 'Mountains'. Emeli also came up with 'Lifetime' for *X Factor* singer Cher Lloyd – a track that Lloyd didn't release and also ended up on Sandé's album. Cowell would later declare that Emeli was his 'favourite songwriter of the minute' – something that didn't necessarily work in her favour. 'It's nice to know but we have never actually met,' was her rather cool response when asked about Cowell's patronage in the *Daily Star*. 'I've had contact through his people but we haven't actually been introduced.'

Emeli would also later have more Cowell-related US success with the song 'Side Effects of You', the title track of the fourth album by *American Idol* winner Fantasia Barrino – she won the third series of the show when Simon Cowell was still on the panel of judges. The album went to No 2 on the Billboard charts – a considerable achievement for both Emeli and Barrino.

Meanwhile, other key songs were being squirreled away for Emeli's first album for Virgin; she wanted her songwriting imprint to be on every track. Her chief collaborator would be Naughty Boy but experienced producer Mike Spencer – who'd worked with artists from soul singer Beverley Knight to Aussie pop princess Kylie Minogue – was brought in to help with one track called 'Heaven'. It was soon earmarked as a single, displacing 'Daddy' as the favoured choice to launch Emeli as a solo artist. Spencer had also produced Newton Faulkner's track 'Teardrop', a cover of an influential track by Bristol trip hop pioneers Massive Attack. The influence of Massive Attack would seemingly seep into the Sandé track too.

The majority of the groundwork for the album was done in Khan's studio in Ealing and many tracks were recorded using a microphone he'd bought with his *Deal or No Deal* winnings. 'Before I met Emeli, I think my approach was forever changing, but Emeli was the first songwriter that I met,' Kahn later told *Sound on Sound* about his approach to formulating the tracks on the album. 'Until then, I'd worked with rappers, so I think writing the songs on her album with her did change my whole approach, especially in terms of musicality. I stopped sampling then. People always ask me how it works, but it just does! I think trust is an important part of it, especially when you're a producer and an artist and you're writing together. I think you've got to be able to trust the person. That's how you learn and we both trust and learn from each other... We do definitely [disagree] sometimes, but it will mostly be something like Emeli will say, "OK, we need to change the chords there" and I'll be thinking, no, we need to keep it that way! But we agree to try everything and we always agree after trying everything.'

One thing that wasn't up for discussion was the opportunity to work with her childhood heroine – Alicia Keys. Following the support slot at the Royal Albert Hall, Sandé was shipped off to America to meet and write with Keys, at the singer's Chelsea studios in New York. 'Working with Alicia Keys was incredible,' she told music writer John Dingwall. 'It was the best trip of my life. She championed me in magazines, which is amazing because I love her. She got in touch to say she wanted me to come and write with her. So I flew out and we got on super well. I felt like I had made a great friend by the end of the week. We wrote a lot just on piano, this amazing Steinway. People like Alicia Keys are a massive inspiration, so it's like a dream come true. She is at the top of her game. Arriving in New York, I was like, don't dry out. Come up with a good idea. I was worried it would be rubbish and I'd be with Alicia Keys.'

'I have to say,' Keys stated on Capital FM, 'myself and Emeli Sandé – when we met and we really began to write together, it was instant magic and that doesn't happen all the time.' The result was a song with the very Sandé-esque title of 'Hope' that would later appear on *Our Version of Events*. The favour would later be returned with Emeli contributing to the tracks 'Not Even the King','Brand New Me' and '101' on Keys' album *Girl on Fire*.

Emeli's visits to New York in the early part of her career would be marked by a piece of jewellery that she still wears to this day. 'I have this ring that I always wear,' she told MTV. 'I got it in Washington Heights one of the first times I came and wrote in New York, so it kind of has special meaning to me. It just reminds me of how I felt at that point. Just so excited to be in New York. Nobody knew who I was, but it was just such a kind of buzz that I got.'

In June 2011, it was finally time for the all-new Emeli Sandé to step out on her own. 'Virgin Records is very proud to announce the much anticipated debut single by Emeli Sandé, a new artist who as a writer has been behind some of the biggest UK hits of 2010,' said the record company press release, headlined INTRODUCING EMELI SANDÉ. 'The first single from the 24-year-old from Aberdeen in Scotland is "Heaven", a euphoric feel good summer track featuring Emeli's subtle yet soaring vocals which will be released on 15 August.'

For Emeli, the key difference was that she would no longer be receiving second billing to another artist – there was no 'featuring' before her name. She was on her own. 'It feels really exciting but it's also added pressure not featuring on anything,' she told MTV. 'I'm more excited than nervous but that is part of it as well. It's amazing to hear the song on the radio. The first time I heard it I was in a taxi at like 2am – it was incredible. I really want to hear it in a club and have a little dance to it.'

If there's was one thing about Sandé's first single that was geared to get people to 'have a little dance', it was the presence of the famed 'Funky Drummer' loop that underpinned the single. It's a sample from the James Brown song of the same name and is one of the – if not the – most sampled pieces of music of all time, played by drummer Clyde Stubblefield. Everyone from Public Enemy to the Beastie Boys has used the rhythm. Its overexposure had meant that people had steered clear of it for several years. Now Sandé and Naughty Boy were resurrecting it. BBC producer Muslim Alim, who'd received Sandé's earliest demo, believes that it was a key reason behind her success. 'Music is cyclical and break beats were coming back,' he told me. 'Just listening to it as a punter – that was the sound that had been missing from dance music for at least a decade. It had become unfashionable yet she went back to it. It has that Massive Attack feel to it.'

Many people would cite Massive Attack – particularly the 1991 hit 'Unfinished Sympathy' as a key inspiration for the track. It was all there: the clattering beats, the lush strings, the uplifting vocal... even the video for 'Heaven' looks like 'Unfinished Sympathy'. It was directed by Jake Nava, probably best known for his 'Single Ladies' and 'Crazy on Love' promos for Beyoncé. The video had the usual shots of urban youth, graffiti and overhead tube trains, but there was also a great deal of religious imagery in the shape of churches, cemeteries and sunlight blasting through the clouds. 'The lyrics are very personal,' Emeli said in a short, behind-the-scenes video made to accompany the single. 'It was something that was inspired by a conversation with Naughty Boy in the studio. We hadn't done any work all day and we were speaking about religion and what it meant to be good. He said at the end of the day, you just have to keep your heart clean. "Heaven" is a confessional piece. I mess up every day but I try every day. There's still hope, we can try again tomorrow.'

The main focus of the video was very firmly Sandé herself, her face raised to the heaven of the title. She's wearing simple black clothes throughout, plus the pendant given to her by her boyfriend's family. For many people it was their first glimpse of the now famous peroxide quiff. It sounded like 'Scottish Adele', but it sure didn't look like her. 'My favourite line in the song is "You're not going to like me, I'm nothing like before," said Naughty Boy. 'I think that sums up the whole thing – everyone changes.'

Rather than shy away from the similarities between 'Heaven' and 'Unfinished Sympathy', Sandé chose to embrace the inspiration the track takes from Massive Attack. 'I'm a big fan,' she confessed to the *Norwich Evening News*. 'I don't think the song is lyrically or melodically that similar, but because the "Funky Drummer" loop has been used so much and it has strings on, people do make the connection. I don't mind though: the whole Bristol movement was really exciting, so I'm actually glad if people get the same vibe from the song. It just started as a late night

Above: Adele Sandé as she looked while she was a student in Glasgow.

Below: Searching for a new groove: an early publicity picture taken while Emeli was working with Souljawn Records.

© *Megan Ansdell*

Left: The normally camera shy Naughty Boy – or Shahid Khan – Emeli's key collaborator on the album *Our Version of Events*.

© *Getty Images*

Right: A star in the making, I ould cocoa. Performing at Koko Camden in November 2011.

© *Rex Features*

At the Opening Ceremony of the
2012 Olympic Games in London,
performing 'Abide With Me'...
© *Getty Images*

Above: ...and at the Closing Ceremony... Performing her version of Professor Green's 'Read All About It' on 12 August.

Inset: At the MOBO Awards on 5 October 2011 with the good Professor himself.

Below: Performing with Labrinth – aka Timothy McKenzie – at a charity gig in London on 10 November 2012.

© Rex Features

Left: A thoughtful Emeli Sandé at a 20th anniversary memorial service for murder victim Stephen Lawrence on 22 April 2013.

Right: The finale of *American Idol* on 16 May 2013 in Los Angeles. Emeli came out to join finalist Amber Holcomb in a version of 'Next to Me' from *Our Version of Events*.   © *Getty Images*

Above: With husband Adam Gouraguine in October 2012. The couple had married the previous month, having been together since their schooldays.

© *Getty Images*

Left: Receiving an honorary doctorate from Glasgow university in Scotland on 11 June 2013.

© *Rex Features*

An incredible year heads towards its conclusion as Emeli Sandé looks totally at home in a packed Royal Albert Hall in London, backed by a band including an all-female string section on 11 November 2012.

© Rex Features

conversation really. Naughty Boy, the producer I work with all the time, had a beat running in the background, I got the first line, and it started from there. I love how songs like that develop: before we knew it we were putting strings on with a synth, Naughty Boy suggested the "Funky Drummer" loop and it came together really organically.'

Reviewers were overwhelmingly impressed by the sound of the single, the musical nods to the past and by Emeli's vocals. 'With 90s drum'n'bass beats and rich horn blasts, "Heaven" sounds both retro and contemporary, fitting snugly alongside recent singles by Yasmin and Katy B,' said the *Guardian*. 'Anchoring the whole thing is Sandé's voice, which seems to be on the edge of delirious, rich with emotion but cracking in all the right places.'

'The singer songwriter has literally featured across every big UK album release within the last few months providing choruses for the likes of Pro Green and Tinie Tempah,' pointed out the Urban Development website. 'She also lent her vocals for Wiley's "Never Be Your Woman" and Chipmunk's "Diamond Rings". Emeli Sandé finally delivers her first single off the back of writing and working with various artists before her own project. The Scottish singer has gone straight for the jugular on her debut as Massive Attack meets James Brown's "Funky Drummer".'

The Digital Spy website was also well and truly on

board: 'Having teased us with her vocal chops on tracks with Chipmunk, Wiley, Tinchy and Professor Green, the question is, can she handle the spotlight alone with her first solo offering? Judging by "Heaven", it's a crime that she didn't put her solo career into action years ago. The result sounds like a lost club classic from the '90s, though by the time the euphoric, string-laden chorus kicks in, you'll be too busy with your fists in the air to notice.'

The reviews were born out by the single's performance in the charts – it got to No 2, only held off the top spot by Wretch 32's 'Don't Go'. The 'Heaven' package was backed up by 'Kill the Boy', an acoustic track that details how badly Emeli's man is going to take the news of their break-up, and 'Easier in Bed', a song that would appear on *Our Version of Events*. Just to show it was all sweetness and light in the world of urban music, Emeli and Wretch 32 released a free download of a collaborative song called 'Underdog Law' at the same time as their respective singles occupied the top two chart spots. 'I don't think that artists at No 1 and No 2 in the charts have ever done this before,' Wretch 32 told the *Sun*. 'Because we're competing, people wanted us to slag each other off. But we respect each other musically and decided to go into the studio together. This is for the love – and for the fans.'

For Emeli, the glowing reviews meant that any

concerns over her stepping out from behind other artists had been unfounded. 'I was so excited,' she told *Lowdown*. 'It meant so much in terms of my confidence because my album wasn't out yet, and no matter how happy you are with a new record, there will always be doubts lurking somewhere. I'd spent so long behind the scenes writing for other people and featuring on other people's records so it just felt so good to get the acknowledgement for me as an artist in my own right.'

On the week of the single's release, Emeli returned to her old school to perform the song in the gym of Alford Academy. With dad Joel acting as DJ she came into the gym after being greeted outside the school by pupils and a piper. Sandé performed 'Clown' on the school's upright piano before segueing into 'Heaven'. Comparing the performance to her support slot for Alicia Keys, she told the *Daily Record*: 'The Royal Albert Hall with Alicia was amazing – it was my dream come true. But I was probably more nervous about singing in front of all the children. I just love the peacefulness here. Everything is calm and relaxing. It's good to get away from all hustle and bustle of big cities. All the lochs and the scenery up here are just amazing. Everything kind of feels the same, I've got so many great memories from my time here. I was already writing songs when I was a pupil here and my music teachers encouraged me to sing in class and in school shows.'

The performance of 'Heaven' made quite an impression on the children at Alford Academy. Hearing the single made quite an impression on a few other people too. Urban Scot and BBC presenter Laura McCrum: I was driving to work and I heard her on the radio. It was "Heaven". I had to pull over. I wanted grab hold of her and go, "Yes! You've done it!"'

The sound and approach was very different to the singer the Urban Scot team had known and nurtured in Scotland – it was far removed from the Neo Soul of old. 'I used to be a music puritan,' says Laura McCrum. 'I used to say, "I hate pop music and mainstream music." But I've never been concerned for Emeli because I don't think she's ever written something or sung something or produced something that isn't what she was interested in. She's in a bigger market now and has more access to larger scale production, different musicians. So I was really quite excited to hear "Heaven" – it reminded me of Goldie, Portishead and "Unfinished Sympathy". It's got that same feel to it with the strings. I'm not going to criticise someone and say, "Oh you've gone mainstream – you're just doing what The Man says." The bottom line is she's a phenomenal talent and sometimes you have to put a track out there that the majority of people will listen to.'

John Ansdell, the man who'd lost out to Virgin, also remembers hearing 'Heaven' for the first time. It was, he says, the moment he realised how far the Emeli he knew had come. And what might have been: 'I did have that "moment",' he told me, when I asked him if it had ever really hit home how he'd missed out on Emeli's success. 'It was when "Heaven" was released. It was very different to anything we'd done before. It was an amazing first track. I was playing table tennis with my friend in the Kelvin Hall in Glasgow. It's a huge place and it's got a pretty good speaker system. I thought, bloody hell, she's really, really made it! And since then she's surpassed it with everything she's done.'

Seven

We're Gonna Do It How We Do It

On the run-up to the release of Emeli's album, a series of events conspired to create anastonishing buzz about the singer. It was all part of the plan. A masterstroke was securing a slot on the BBC show *Later with Jools Holland*. Since it had started in 1992, Holland's show was the go-to place if you wanted to showcase an emerging talent. Alongside Sandé for that episode were the polite rockers Snow Patrol, electronic Swedish band Little Dragon and the hippie troubadour Roy Harper. Introducing Emeli, Holland told viewers: 'Our next artist is from Aberdeen. She's written songs and helped with songs for all sorts of people. But now, I'm delighted that she's here doing songs for herself. We welcome: Emeli Sandé.'

There was little by way of frills for Emeli's performance of 'Heaven' on *Later* – just her voice, acoustic guitar, cello and percussion. A less familiar track at that stage, 'Next to Me', was also performed and got the same stripped-down treatment. It mirrored the way her management wanted her to be viewed as a live performer: provide as little distraction as possible, then people will concentrate on the voice. 'As people saw her, they realised what an act it was and that it was real,' Emeli's manager Adrian Sykes told journalist Jan Blumentrath. 'We didn't cloak it in lots of production and lots of instrumentation. It was all about her, a guitarist and a cello player. The band thing was the next level for us. There was a natural progression.'

For those who'd known about Emeli's talent for some time, the planets were lining up for the singer. Urban Scot's David Craig: 'Alicia Keys had tweeted about her. She did Jools Holland. At that point I thought, my God this is really going to happen for her. This is about to get real. Once you're asked on Jools Holland – that's a defining moment for anybody, that was one of the benchmarks. She was getting a lot of play on the radio and that's when I thought, she's arrived.'

The following month Sandé returned to Jools

Holland's show with all the bells and whistles to perform 'Read All About It' – the single with Professor Green that would be another key part of her pre-album build-up. It also served as the lead single for his new album. 'Read All About It' turned both Sandé and Green into No 1 artists, and it gave Sandé a more distinct urban edge, something that her somewhat strait-laced image had occasionally lacked. 'Working with him [Green] I've noticed younger fans, even kids [at shows],' she told the *Sun*. 'When you write for Susan Boyle and go on Jools you expect an older audience. But I want to reach everyone and cover different audiences. I write as honestly as I can. I'm not cool, I don't fit into any genre.'

'Read All About It' did not have the most commercial of subject matters. Professor Green's father committed suicide in 2008 and the rapper had to identify his body, later citing this as the moment that made him turn his life around. Since then Green had been accused in the press by his stepmother of using the incident to bolster his fame and 'Read All About It' was his response. 'I guess with the subject matter it's not really a chart-friendly track,' he told MTV. 'It's not what people would normally talk about on a pop song. But ultimately it kind of does fit. It's got quite a lot of commercial appeal despite the subject matter. The song is entirely autobiographical. It's all about situations that I've been through and continue to go through. The meaning for me is just being entirely upfront and honest. You know, knowing what's out there and just saying to people, "It's there, here I am." I say in the song, "I won't censor myself for anyone. All that is good, all that is bad, all it is me… and by that I just mean to say, take me as I am – I'm imperfect."'

The subject matter may not have been aimed at the charts but the soaring chorus – sung by Sandé – most certainly was and Green was quick to praise Emeli's performance. 'Emeli Sandé was the only vocalist that could've worked on that song. No one else would've been able to convey that emotion and she absolutely killed it.'

The video to accompany the track featured a look-alike child actor playing the young Professor as well as epic, backlit shots of both Green and Emeli – it showcased Emeli just as much as it showed off the main artist. On 28 October 2011, the track went to No 1, a major achievement for both Green and Emeli. 'It's incredible,' Emeli told theofficialcharts.com on hearing the single had gone to the top of the charts. 'It shows a change in what people want to hear. People do want to hear truth in music and honesty. That made it really important to me.'

An indication of how she was seeping into the national consciousness came in November when she gave an unusual performance at a school in Glasgow.

Emeli joined children at Howford School in Crookston, Glasgow, for a music therapy lesson run by the Nordoff Robbins charity. She sat in on a session that aimed to help 'challenged' youngsters use music to help learning and social skills and played them some songs on an upright piano. When she had finished, one of the pupils stood up and sang a word-perfect version of 'Heaven'. 'That was amazing,' she said, as he finished singing. 'It's very moving to see how powerful music can be and it was really special to see how using music can activate different skills. It was very simple yet incredibly effective. The kids were amazing and it was astonishing to see just how the music gets to them straight away.' Sandé and the Nordoff Robbins organisation would go on to enjoy a long relationship and she would sing at the charity's annual Christmas carol service in London the following year.

Meanwhile, in addition to her own shows, it was announced that Sandé would be the support act for Coldplay's UK stadium tour, a brilliant coup that would put the singer in front of thousands of people outside her immediate fan base. As luck would have it, the first date of the tour was on familiar territory. 'The first show we did was in Glasgow,' she told Radio 1's *Newsbeat*, 'so that was a home crowd. It's difficult because you think, this is a crowd which came for Coldplay – how will they react to my music?'

The reaction was overwhelmingly positive, so much so that the band invited Sandé on the US leg of the tour too. Coldplay lead singer Chris Martin was the driving force behind the choice of Emeli – not an obvious act to support the stadium rockers. 'He heard the music and he heard what I was about as a musician and from that, just kind of brought me on board,' she told Boombox.com in an interview to promote her US shows. 'So we did the European tour with them, which was incredible. I'm just really honoured to be asked to come back and introduce my music over here [in America] with them. He's great. The whole band was welcoming to us and I had a fantastic time. So I'm very excited about this summer. Coming back and doing even bigger shows is going to be incredible.'

Always the student, Emeli watched Coldplay from the side of the stage and learned a few lessons in the art of entertaining a massive crowd. 'When you watch them onstage it's so energetic, but there's still an intimacy to it,' she said. 'So I guess I've learned that from them, and there's such discipline going on with them behind the scenes. Everything is very considered and everybody is very welcome and those are things I'll take with me for the rest of my career. I've had a few conversations with Chris [Martin] and I see them when they're coming on and I'm going off, but the main thing I've learned from them is seeing them onstage and how it all operates.'

Everything was going Sandé's way and her manager couldn't have been more delighted. 'Suddenly we had this building momentum of great press, great live reviews, records on the radio,' he told the hitquarters website. 'People having seen her on TV and then with all of that, we got a No 1 through her feature on the Professor Green record. At the end of the year Emeli [was nominated for] the Brits Critics' Choice award. My hope had always been that we'd get a nomination, because essentially that's recognition from the industry saying that Emeli is going to be the one for the next year.'

There would be more good news to report at the event to announce who had been nominated for the Brits – though it didn't necessarily bring the kind of attention that Emeli would have wanted. On the red carpet, journalists had noticed Emeli's engagement ring. Adam had proposed to her at the MOBO awards in Glasgow, but the pair had decided to keep it secret. But now the news was out that she planned to marry and she looked uncomfortable as reporters began trying to coax a few words from her about their plans. 'He's a scientist so this whole world... he doesn't want to be involved,' she said when asked about her fiancé. The discomfort continued as she was asked to flash the ring for the benefit of the cameras. When was the big day? 'No plans for a wedding just yet,' was her swift reply before moving down the line of reporters... only to be asked about it all over again.

The one blip in her career could have been Sandé's second single. Released in late November, 'Daddy' had been one of the first songs that Sandé and Naughty Boy had written together when their partnership began. It had been earmarked for her debut before 'Heaven' took on the task. Producer Naughty Boy got a 'featuring' credit, though the casual listener wouldn't be able to spot his direct contribution. The song had the same clattering break beats and big strings of 'Heaven' but lacked the killer chorus. It was backed up by half a dozen remixes but the song didn't feel as omnipresent on the radio as its predecessor and perhaps as a result only reached No 21 in the charts.

The accompanying video saw Sandé take a swing at a little acting instead of the usual performance piece – bear in mind her opinion of herself as being a better singer than actress after she'd tried musical theatre at university. In the 'Daddy' video she's the girlfriend of a bad guy who's an armed robber and drug addict. 'Daddy is about addiction,' Emeli later revealed in a mini-documentary that accompanied the release of her album. 'Everyone is essentially addicted to something and it fascinates me. I think that's why I enjoyed studying neurology because we are all flawed in some way, whether it comes from our personalities or a genetic link.'

Just to prove that there's no such thing as a golden touch, November also saw the release of the debut album by a girl group called Parade. The five-piece was a mish-mash of actresses, *The X Factor* entrants and previous girl band members, and their self-titled debut included a song called 'Rokstar', written by Emeli and Naughty Boy. It was buried at the back end of an album that only got to No 171 in the charts, but it's a hidden gem – a growling tale of loneliness from a bright and breezy act that was essentially The Saturdays with a different name.

Meanwhile, all the elements were in place for Emeli's album. First there was the matter of a title. 'I was staying with the producer that I worked with [Naughty Boy], we were having breakfast, and people were asking me what the title of the album is,' she told journalist Chris Azzopardi. 'Then we were being told you have to play by these rules in the industry – you have to do this, that and the other. He said, "Well, this is our version of events, so we're gonna do it how we do it." I loved that defiance. These were stories I wanted to tell; they were stories that we thought maybe other people would want told for them, to give a voice to people who might not feel represented on radio. It just sounded like the perfect title of the album. This is our version of events, and maybe I can speak for other people through my stories.'

The album that contained those stories – *Our Version*

of Events – was released in February 2012. It was a slick, carefully presented package. Tasteful black-and-white pictures by Russian-born art-house photographer Alexandra Catiere were there alongside childhood snaps of Emeli, pictures of her parents and stock images of Nina Simone and Billie Holiday. The cover shot was a mysterious affair, concentrating largely on the back of Sandé's head.

The album inside – 14 tracks in its initial incarnation – kicks off in familiar territory with the stirring strings and funky drums of 'Heaven'. Making sure the casual listener isn't frightened off by the unfamiliar is a common opening gambit in track listings. For the purposes of the song, heaven isn't a metaphor – to Sandé, it was a reality. 'I definitely believe in God and I believe in heaven, although I don't follow religion,' she told the *Daily Mirror*. '"Heaven" was about trying to be good. My idea of heaven? A lot of music, somewhere very calm. I felt it at Christmas with the family around. Kids are so pure and innocent, and one was learning the piano. It reminded me of when I was learning.'

'My Kind of Love' – later a single – is up next. It starts like a track from the 'lost' *Have You Heard?* album: Sandé, plus piano, plus beats. It soon opens up into a more widescreen affair and it becomes apparent this is a more generic track. It's one of the few tracks on the initial version of the album that doesn't involve

Naughty Boy – the chief co-writer is US hip hop producer Emile Haynie, who'd previously worked with the likes of Eminem (on *Recovery*) and Kanye West. Producer, writer and arranger Daniel Tannenbaum and remixers Craze and Hoax – aka Harry Craze and Hugo Chegwin – were also involved. The song, which could just as easily have been sung by Beyoncé as Sandé, came from Emeli's trip to the US before she quit university. 'When I had some free time in New York I went to see Emile Haynie, and he gave me a load of beats to take back,' she later explained to Q magazine. 'I was in the kitchen with my sister listening to the tunes and the song just came to me out of nowhere really. It was definitely a natural one to write.'

Much more quirky and individualistic are the two minutes and 11 seconds that come next. 'Where I Sleep' is a rum mix of music-box plinks, beats – a nod to Michael Jackson's 'Ain't No Sunshine' – and synth. It could be considered throwaway, but it's heartfelt 'home is where the heart is' message feels honest. The story behind it is charming in its ordinariness. 'I was on tour in Scotland,' she later revealed, 'and I was in my hotel room with my stylist and we were just having a girly chat. She said that when she got back home with one of her boyfriends, it really felt like, that's where I sleep – and I just loved that phrase. Like it doesn't matter where you are in the world, you always know that's where your home is.'

The story of the next track, 'Mountains', is well documented and to bring the point home, the lyrics to the song were accompanied by a picture of Emeli's parents Joel and Diane at their wedding. Detailing their struggles in Sunderland – and their desire to move to a place where people are 'less crazy' – it's a grim but ultimately positive tale, something of a Sandé motif. 'I am quite positive,' she told Radio 2 in 2012. 'I have always found comfort and strength in music and lyrics and I definitely wanted to put the best part of me forward if you were going to listen to it over and over again. I want to be as honest as possible but I want the listener to be left with a sense of hope or a sense that things can change or that something is left in this world that can be forever or is unchangeable.'

'Mountains' was one of the songs that Emeli had had to fight to keep for herself when she began as a songwriter, and so was the next track, 'Clown'. This was a song that would become a single and something of a Sandé signature track. Music industry veteran Grant Mitchell – who's worked with everyone from Gary Barlow to Bob the Builder – is also credited on the track. 'This is about the industry and the struggle to get into it,' she explained to journalist Gavin Martin at the time of the album's release. 'But I was also thinking about Jeremy Kyle's show a lot when I wrote that – how we kind of laugh at these people on our TV screens who are desperate enough to go on and talk about their problems. It was written very quickly – in two or three hours. I wanted it to be defiant... I'm going to be your clown, but I'll still have the guts to put myself out there.'

The kitchen-sink drama of 'Daddy' works far better in the context of an album than it did as a standalone single – '"Daddy" is about obsession and addiction,' she later explained to Q magazine. 'It signifies the one thing you keep going back to. People who are quite artistic usually get obsessive over very small things that aren't really conducive to what they need to do. I don't really know why I called it "Daddy" to be honest. I guess when you're young your dad is the one who sets the boundaries in your life, and is in control to a certain point.'

Next up is 'Maybe', a track that actually pre-dates her writing partnership with Naughty Boy and is therefore something of a curio. 'I wrote this [in 2009] before I met Shahid, with Paul Herman. He wrote with Dido and had just worked with Jessie J. It's just about confusion. Do we ever know for sure when we break up with someone that they weren't the love of our life? There's always a question whether you've made the right decision.' 'Maybe' has the big strings and the peaks and troughs you'd expect, but lacks some of the character of the Khan tracks.

'Suitcase' is a classic 'my baby's leaving me' song,

based around a twisty, country-and-western guitar lick by regular Sandé guitarist Ben Harrison. The riff is so central to the song that Harrison earned himself a credit. The song – originally the words were 'blue face' – was inspired by a major bust-up Sandé had gone through with her boyfriend Adam Gouraguine. 'I got to the studio and Shahid had this guitar piece and my sister was there. I was singing, "He's got a blue face…" and I thought it sounded like "suitcase". Then this whole story came out. Thinking back, maybe I was trying to express how I was feeling, subconsciously almost. We [Adam and Emeli] had a fall-out a month or two before that. It was an uneasy time and I was writing about that.'

Ben Harrison's finger-picking guitar style was to the fore on the next song, 'Breaking the Law' – not to be confused with the heavy metal song of the same name by Judas Priest. It's actually an 'I'd do anything for you' song for and about Emeli's sister Lucy. It's just Harrison's guitar and Sandé's voice, less than three minutes long, but the track merits repeated listening; it draws you back time and time again.

The public would get repeated opportunities to listen to the next track when it was released as a single at the same time as the album came out. 'Next to Me' would be a No 2 hit in the UK and also marked Sandé's first dent in the US charts, as well as European markets like Poland, Finland and Ireland. 'I wanted that old soul feel to this one. I wanted to speak of love and loyalty, and to celebrate good men. This is about God... or your man.' The stripped-down, old school feel extended to the video too – essentially Sandé and a drummer in an old warehouse, playing with a revivalist, gospel-edged passion. 'I wrote this in my bedroom,' she said. 'I wanted a song that was very simple in its idea, having someone next to you, that's the bottom line. I was inspired by early Aretha Franklin and soul music. We wanted big drums and pianos. I think it will go down really well at a festival.'

The next track, 'River', was at the top of the list when it came to the lengthy dedications on the album: 'To my river. Your love is nothing that I have earned. Thank you for all of these dreams. Refresh and gladden my spirit and give me the strength and the humility to one day find the sea.' The song was written in one sitting, just Sandé and a piano, which is largely how it's presented here, barring some tasteful string and choir arrangements. It's another song with an unabashed religious edge: 'I feel as if I wrote the song "River" about God,' Emeli later told Radio 2. 'It's a journey. I'm still trying to find the sea, find the right answers. But I think if you listen to that voice that feels right which I believe to be God, that's your river. And it will take you where you need to go.'

'Lifetime' has that familiar funky drummer feel – actually a nod to US band Little Feat – and a two-note piano motif. That means it doesn't really stand out from other Sandé tracks, and it tails off slightly apologetically before the three minute mark – it's definitely an album track. '"Lifetime" is about everything changing. I guess it has a similar sentiment to "Where I Sleep", and it's about something that you'll love forever,' she told music writer Joe Bishop. 'For me that's music, for others it might be something else. The industry that we're in moves so fast, things can change within a week or two and you never quite know where you stand.'

'Hope' is the track that Sandé wrote with Alicia Keys. The American star also gets a producer credit and she played and programmed keyboards and drums on the track too. It's a 'list song' – the two women decided to put down all the things that they hoped for the world. The song namechecks Martin Luther King Jr and has that earnest feel common to a lot of Keys's work. 'She's really awesome, very down to earth but very focused,' Sandé said at the time. 'Knows how to get a good song done.'

The original version of the album tails out with 'Read All About It (Pt III)' – a sequel of sorts to the Professor Green track she'd guest-starred on. 'People keep asking me about Part II and even I don't know where it is!' she told Q magazine. 'Apparently there is one, though.' In fact Green recorded Part II for none other than Q magazine. 'Professor Green did his version last year which was great, and I wanted to think about what my version of the song was – how can I make it personal? And that's what I loved about it, how personal it was.'

For *Our Version of Events*, Sandé takes Green's angry rap about his treatment by the media and turns it into an apparent tribute to writing partner Naughty Boy – even referencing the title of the album. It's Sandé back to her roots – just her and a piano.

The reviews of the album weren't as overwhelmingly positive as history and the later success of *Our Version of Events* might make us believe. The good ones, however, were very good indeed. 'She's made an album that deserves to linger in the limelight,' said Q magazine. 'Passionate, powerful and possessed of real star quality.'

'*Our Version of Events* often sounds like an album operating on two levels,' said the *Daily Telegraph*, 'with songs that flourish on a tension between rawness and polished craft. This is a hugely impressive introduction to a dynamic, arresting talent. Chances are it'll make her a star.'

The *Observer* held Emeli's songwriting work for Simon Cowell acts like Leona Lewis and Susan Boyle against her – along with the fact that Cowell had declared Sandé his favourite songwriter. 'Not all that many half-Zambian Scottish former neuroscience students work in pop music... Even fewer declare Virginia Woolf as an influence and fewer still have a ~~giant tattoo of Frida Kahlo down one arm. There is~~ such a great deal to commend singer Emeli Sandé. If her peroxide quiff stands visually for Sandé's unconventionality, the title of her album, *Our Version of Events*, promises perspective, too... Ultimately, though, her version of events could have been so much more intriguing... her album has a preternaturally middle-aged, middle-of-the-road feel. It's understandable, given Sandé's Cowell connections. But it is regrettable. You can hear Leona Lewis singing too many of these songs. And while that's good for Sandé's future prospects as a songwriter, it's a waste of her idiosyncrasies.'

The *NME* – not a natural home for Sandé – flagged up the album's obvious influences and begrudgingly gave credit to Emeli's skills as a songwriter, although they credited her as being from the wrong city. 'Pop has a curious way of repeating itself in 20-year cycles,' the review said. 'In 2011, for example, Glaswegian singer-songwriter Emeli Sandé released "Heaven", a song that didn't so much borrow the template from Massive Attack's "Unfinished Sympathy" as lift it wholesale. It did produce a great pop song, though, and this is the crux of Sandé's debut. Original it is not – there's little here that couldn't have come straight off a Shara Nelson album – but she does write some fine tunes, including new single "Next To Me", a rollicking piano stomper currently eating up your radio. She could ease back on sincere acoustic numbers like "Breaking The Law" though (no, not that one), which turn the tail end into a bit of a slog.'

A week after its release, *Our Version of Events* went straight into the charts at No 1, knocking Lana Del Rey off the top slot and pushing 'London Adele' into third. 'It wasn't close to anything I'd imagined,' Emeli told Clare Balding when asked about the suddenness and intensity of the album's success. 'I wanted to release my album and I wanted it to go into the Top 5 and that was all I had planned to be honest.'

Seasoned Sandé-watchers like Urban Scot's David Craig weren't surprised that the content of the album was still recognisably by the singer he knew in Glasgow – but it was still a world away from the kind of songs Emeli had written for other artists. 'I think she was always clear that anything she would release would not be anything like that,' he told me. 'She wasn't willing to water down the stuff she wanted to put out. I'm sure the label wanted to push her in certain directions and I wouldn't imagine she got 100 per cent of what she wanted, but her first album sounded a lot like the old stuff she was doing, so she didn't stray too far from the things that she loved. The success is a testament to her as a person and as an artist, that she managed to stick to her guns.'

Eight

They Didn't Know
I Was in Both

The 2012 Brit Awards would become notorious for
an incident at the end of the show when Adele –
'London Adele', that is – was cut short by presenter
James Corden as she accepted her award for Album of
the Year. The previous year Adele had stunned the
audience into silence with her rendition of 'Someone
Like You'. By 2012 she was queen of everything she
surveyed, but that didn't stop Brit organisers from
forcing Corden to get her off the stage so Blur could
play. Adele gave organisers the middle finger for
spoiling what should have been a triumphant
moment for British music.

As it happens, another Adele – 'Scottish Adele' –

suffered a similar fate at the Brits in 2012. She'd been nominated for Best Breakthrough Award as well as the Brits Critics' Choice Award. She was an outside bet for Best Breakthrough – Ed Sheeran was where the clever money was – but the second nomination was a sure sign she was on her way, as previous Critics' Choice winners had included Jessie J, Ellie Goulding, Florence + The Machine and, in 2008, 'London Adele' herself.

Emeli's family had travelled down from Alford to see their daughter get her award and the singer had performed for Brit organisers and journalists at a pre-show dinner. But when it came time for the show itself, the opportunity for Emeli to make a speech was nowhere to be seen – it had been cut from the running order due to 'time restraints'. Previous winners like Jessie J had been given time to say a few words of thanks – but not Emeli. Not only was she not allowed to speak, she wasn't even permitted to go on stage to receive the award. When the time came when Emeli should have been speaking, viewers instead saw Jessie J explaining why the award was so important and giving Sandé some career advice – as Emeli sat in the audience with her parents Joe and Diane. So much for time restraints.

The story was overshadowed in many parts of the media because of the incident at the end of the show with Adele – but not in Scotland: BLUNDERING BRIT AWARD BOSSES LEAVE SCOTS SINGER IN TEARS AFTER SPEECH

SNUB screamed the headline in the *Daily Record*, a long-time supporter of Sandé and her career. 'EXCLUSIVE: Scots singer Emeli Sandé broke down in tears when she was hit by a huge snub at the Brit awards, we can reveal,' the story went on. The paper quoted a 'source close to the devastated singer' as saying: 'I just think it was an almighty cock-up. I don't think it was deliberate. They dropped the ball on Emeli. She received very poor treatment. She has a No 1 album and they're asking Jessie J what advice she has got for her. Emeli's family were there and this was the moment when she should have been celebrating and having a nice time. Instead of talking to Jessie J, they should have been talking to Emeli at her table. After all the hard work of the last year, she was really looking forward to having it officially acknowledged on the night in front of her family and friends. She wanted to say thanks for the honour and for the support she has received on the way. She is disappointed that she didn't get the opportunity to do that.'

It was also pointed out that presenter James Corden seemed to have plenty of time to interview the likes of Kylie Minogue in the audience – not up for any award that year – but not Emeli, who had actually won something. She remained quiet over the issue, but a 'source' close to her was quoted in the *Sun* as saying: 'Emeli deserved her moment in the spotlight in front of her peers, the industry and her family. She'd been looking forward to it for months and was really disappointed when her win was not properly recognised.'

Brit organisers were sorry – but Emeli hardly got the full public apology that 'London Adele' got. 'Because there was more music than ever before, everything got pushed back,' a spokesman said. 'The Brits love Emeli. They really support her and think she's fantastic.'

'Nothing can take away from how happy I am about winning the Critics' Choice award,' Emeli said afterwards. 'I was a bit disappointed with the way things went at the event, especially as my family were there too. But my album's No 1, my single's No 2 and I've got loads of stuff going on, so I really have nothing to complain about. I'm so grateful to be in this position and to have this kind of success already. It's all a dream come true.'

But it would not be the only time Emeli Sandé would be dropped from the running order of a major event in 2012.

Meanwhile, Emeli was becoming visible to the point of omnipresence at swanky events north and south of the border. The Scottish Style Awards, the Elle Style Awards, the Prince's Trust Celebrate Success Awards, the *Daily Record* Our Heroes Awards, the Silver Clef Awards – it seemed as if no event was complete with the presence of Emeli Sandé. She also announced her own headlining UK tour, playing everywhere from Aberdeen to Norwich.

March saw Emeli make her North American debut, playing a handful of 'showcase' dates in the US and Canada. Two out of the nine dates were invite-only affairs for the benefit of the American music industry, so they could see what the fuss was about before her album was given a US release in June, and she returned to play more than a dozen shows with Coldplay in July. She also made her US TV debut on the Conan O'Brien show. 'I just wanted to have the opportunity to introduce my music over here,' she told US website Boombox. 'You know I'm really happy with everything that's happening in the UK and now I'm just approaching it like a brand new challenge. I really didn't want any expectations because that's how I've approached everything in the UK and I think that's the best way – just to introduce your music and your stories, slowly… in a more intimate fashion, and then slowly build it like that. So I'm excited and so far I've just been really blown away with people's reactions here and people connecting, so I'm really happy.'

Her first US date at The Box venue in lower Manhattan, New York City, was one of the invite-only shows where she played with the stripped-down cello/guitar/percussion set-up, designed to highlight her voice. 'It's my very first performance in America and I'm so excited to be here and introducing my songs,' she told the audience. 'This is a very small and intimate set so you will able to hear the melodies and lyrics, and both are very important to me.' She played just seven songs, including a cover version of Coldplay's 'Every Teardrop is a Waterfall'.

Reviewing the show was influential US music blogger Arjan Timmermans: 'Once in a very rare while an artist comes along who can move listeners using the combined power of poignant storytelling, timeless melodies and a heartfelt performance,' he told his readers. 'It's an artist who can hit people right at their core with a message of hope and humanity that is universally understood. Emeli Sandé is one of those uniquely gifted singer/songwriters who can let her guard down, effortlessly belt out a tune and emote with such passion that she makes you feel every single emotion in her music from your toes up.'

Another review, this time from the Bloomberg website, must have been exactly the kind of publicity Emeli's team were hoping for: ADELE, ARETHA GET UPSTAGED AS EMELI SANDÉ PLANS INVASION. 'Her first name is Adele, and she's the latest British soul singer to try to conquer the US. She's not Adele Adkins, the multi-Grammy-winner behind "Rolling in the Deep." She's Adele Emeli Sandé, a former medical student who's being compared to Aretha Franklin. Sandé's dropped her first given name, not surprisingly. She still has the voice, the songs and the attitude – with a support slot on Coldplay's North American summer tour. Watching her perform, it's not difficult to fathom Sandé's popularity. A shocking blonde super-size quiff dominates the top of her head. The performance matches the hair. Sandé sounds as though she may have jet engines instead of lungs, all the better for belting out the big choruses she repeatedly rustles up.'

Back in the UK, the press – especially the Scottish press – seized on the reviews as clear evidence that Emeli was about to become the latest singer to 'crack' the American market. The singer herself was more cautious, downplaying what were essentially a handful of showcase gigs. 'We started very slow in America,' she told the *Daily Record*. 'It was small acoustic shows. We played places like Los Angeles, New York and Chicago and everywhere there has been a great reaction. It has been really lovely. They listen to the lyrics and the melody over there and the reaction has been fantastic. It is a good feeling and it feels like it is bubbling. It is a good time to come to America.'

At home, things were a little more down to earth. In May, Emeli and fiancé Adam moved to the east London area of Hackney. The couple became regulars in the London Fields park and at the local Picturehouse cinema, and Emeli joined the local gym. It would be a nice easy trip to work for her when she agreed to play at Radio 1's Big Weekend event in June, a two-day event on Hackney Marshes that attracted 100,000 people. Emeli appeared alongside major acts like Nicki Minaj, Jay-Z and Rhianna. 'I really loved east London since I moved down from Scotland, but other places don't have that community vibe,' told the *Hackney Gazette*. 'We just wanted something that was quite creative, but where there's real life going on and it's not just too posey or too arty,' she said. The couple were planning to get married in a matter of months. Their decision to get married would remain a secret from everyone apart from their closest family and friends until the pair had actually wed.

There was another secret that Emeli had to keep at this time: she had received a call from film director Danny Boyle. The Oscar winner behind *Trainspotting* and *Slumdog Millionaire* had been tasked by the British Government to direct the opening ceremony for the 2012 Olympic Games. He'd been approached about the job in 2010 and at the time it had been seen as something of a thankless task. The 2008 Beijing Games had set the bar impossibly high in terms of cost and ambition, especially its opening ceremony – how could a budget British Games possibly compete? Boyle drafted in a diverse team to help make the show happen: writer Frank Cottrell Boyce – best known for his children's books and for scripting the film *24 Hour Party People* – came on board, along with electronic dance band Underworld. Even the Queen lent a hand as the ultimate Bond girl in a pre-recorded film sequence with actor Daniel Craig.

The opening ceremony was to be held on 27 July 2012 at the Olympic Stadium in east London and was given the title 'Isles of Wonder'. 'It's a challenge, of course, because it can easily be just a cold spectacle – awe-inspiring but not necessarily of the heart,' Boyle later told journalist Hadley Freeman. 'We want the ceremony to have a visceral effect on people, for it to be a collective experience. Stirring emotion is hard in a stadium.'

Nothing stirs emotion quite like music – and that's where Emeli Sandé came in. She explained how she came to be involved in the Olympics in an interview with Clare Balding on Radio 2. 'It was perhaps six months before the opening ceremony and Danny Boyle asked if I could come into the secret Olympic bunker. I didn't know why I had been invited, but they sat us down and showed us this big model of the fields and the big opening scene and they played us the sequencing of events and they said, "We want you to sing 'Abide With Me'," and I just thought, wow, that's perfect. It was a song that was played at my granddad's funeral and it's a song that means a lot to me and to so many people around the world and I just thought it was perfect. I loved how intimate it was.'

'We received a simple email asking whether she wanted to play,' Emeli's manager Adrian Sykes later told *Sound on Sound* magazine. 'All that hard work on the shows and in getting a No 1 album brings you to the position where you might be considered for such a high- profile event. You don't seek out once in a lifetime opportunities, they come to you.'

Other musicians announced for the opening ceremony included Mike Oldfield, Arctic Monkeys and Dizzee Rascal. It was a huge deal for Emeli – made even bigger by the fact that she was accidentally the subject of one of the great showbusiness double-bookings of all time. The artistic director of the closing ceremony, Kim Gavin (the man behind Take That's Circus tour), decided he wanted Emeli for his show too: 'It was by coincidence,' she later admitted to the BBC. 'They didn't know I was in both. We had to say eventually, maybe a couple of weeks afterwards. Kim Gavin asked if I'd be a part of it and open up with "Read All About It", so I was very nervous but felt very honoured to work with such incredible minds, seeing this idea develop in the little room become something that was so important for Britain, to show a new version of our country, was great.'

The Who, Take That and George Michael were also lined up for the closing show, due to take place on 12 August. An Olympic Committee spokesman said: 'It is imperative that the games close in spectacular fashion but that there is substance as well as style. Although a lot of work is going into the production side of things, the committee wanted four major artists representing Great Britain over the past 50 years to headline. Emeli will appeal to youngsters, while The Who are an inspired throwback to the Swinging 60s. Kim has worked with Take That before and the boys, including Robbie Williams, will put on their most dazzling set ever. Finally, George Michael is a global icon and this, for him, will be a major comeback. The gig will be a fitting Olympics send-off.'

Meanwhile, as preparations for the Olympics got into full swing, 'My Kind of Love' was released as Emeli's next single – making it the fourth track from *Our Version of Events* to get a standalone release. The song was a straight-ahead love letter for soon-to-be-husband Adam. 'It was the last song I wrote for the album and it came to me in the kitchen,' she explained to the *Daily Mirror*. 'I'm engaged and this is about my fiancé Adam's unconditional love for me. He's so separate from the industry, and anything I wanted to do – be a doctor, be a musician – he's supported me.'

The message of unconditional love was reinforced by a video to accompany the track showing Sandé busting a childhood friend (played by *Skins* actress Layla Lewis) out of hospital and taking her on a trip to the seaside. Dawn Shadforth – still best known for her first ever video, Kylie Minogue's 'Can't Get You Out of

My Head' – directed the moving piece. It was far better than the usual urban clichés that had featured in some of Emeli's other videos.

Sandé's background in medicine seemed to feed into the hospital-based narrative of the video. 'When it comes to videos, I love working with directors that inspire me visually,' she told the AllHipHop website. 'When I've seen someone's work that's just made me think outside the box – I always love working with people like that in a collaborative way. But specifically for "My Kind of Love", the director and I had a conversation on the phone and I told her the story that had inspired me to write that song. As a [third and fourth year] med student, you go into hospitals and start learning the practice of being a doctor. So even as a med student, you're entrusted with so many personal stories and so many real raw emotions. It was seeing who is there for you when you're in hospital, who actually comes for you when your health has gone – the one thing that we all take for granted. I told a very specific story about a patient I'd met, and then she helped me bring it to life. So, that song's really important to me, and writing it was really special, because vocally I feel like I can really let everything out, and really let that emotion come through; but lyrically I feel it really says exactly what I wanted it to say.'

Despite – or maybe because of – the striking and

different video, the song only reached No 17 in the UK charts.

Meanwhile, *Our Version of Events* was released in the US, and the American critics seemed largely to fall in line with their UK counterparts: they liked the album, they liked Sandé, but they still had reservations. 'It's not a flawless album, but rather one with a number of flawless moments,' pointed out the *New York Times*. 'When she chooses to unleash it, Ms. Sandé has a perspective-altering voice, clear and brassy and weapons-grade. Often, after letting a song build casually – as on "My Kind of Love" and "Breaking the Law" – she explodes at the chorus. Even though she does it several times, it's always unexpected and invigorating.'

'It's filled with finely crafted, expertly produced love songs about complex, complicated emotions (not a single reference to what she bought someone, or what they bought her), as well as songs thickly peppered with social consciousness,' said the *Los Angeles Times*. 'The greatest weakness though is that on many of her socially conscious songs the edges have been buffed away; they're vague and generic enough to be non-threatening, while the listener who sings along can be flattered (or flatter him or herself) that they're saying something profound when they really aren't. But in comparison to the drudge that is contemporary mainstream American pop and R&B, Emeli's folk-inflected soul/pop is Nina Simone and Bob Dylan all in one.'

Declarations of love and support were a little hard to find in the press when it came to the final run-up to the Olympic Games in July. The feel-good factor that occurred after the Olympics had taken place was a far cry from the reality of the headlines prior to the event: overpriced tickets, empty seats, bus strikes, miming symphony orchestras, queues at Heathrow passport control, rocket launchers on tower blocks, security staff scandals, protesting taxi drivers and, to top it all, an Olympic Stadium that had been turned into some kind of Tellytubbyland with sheep, cows and floating rain clouds courtesy of director Danny Boyle. Things didn't look good.

What viewers and the 80,000-strong audience in the stadium got that night was an opening segment so British it was like being repeatedly hit in the face with an open bag of fish and chips. From the opening sequence showing the source of the River Thames to the final notes of Emeli Sandé's performance before the athletes flooded into the stadium, the show stopped the cynics in their tracks. Boyle's vision of a green and pleasant land was literally stripped away as the industrial revolution – led by a beaming Kenneth Branagh as Victorian engineer Isambard Kingdom Brunel – brutally uprooted the old Britain before paving the way for a new, more realistic country that forged the Olympic rings in its manufacturing cauldron. One of the commentators for the ceremony's TV coverage on the BBC was that early Sandé supporter Trevor Nelson: 'This is my kind of history lesson,' he said as NHS workers were celebrated alongside children's literature and Pearly Kings were brought on alongside parachuting Queens.

Music was central to the show and a montage took viewers through another kind of history lesson: a musical one. The Jam, Eric Clapton, The Who, The Rolling Stones, The Kinks, The Beatles, Mud, The Specials, David Bowie, Queen, Sex Pistols, New Order, Frankie Goes to Hollywood, Soul II Soul, Happy Mondays, Eurythmics, Prodigy, Underworld, Blur, Dizzee Rascal, Amy Winehouse, Muse and Tinie Tempah were all put forward as the best of British. The last song of the section was 'Heaven' by Emeli Sandé.

It was time for a change of pace and tone. 'The excitement of that moment in Singapore seven years ago when London won the Games was tempered with great sorrow the very next day, with events on the seventh of July that year,' said BBC commentator Hazel Irvine. 'A moving wall of memories to remember those who are no longer here to share in this wonderful event and this is a calming and reflective pause after the exuberance of the last hour and a quarter.'

Armed with handfuls of dust, choreographer Akram Khan led his troupe of dancers though a piece that was an oasis of simplicity within the bombast of what had come so far. 'I realised I had to be very Japanese about it,' he told journalists after the show when asked to describe the dance. 'When Danny [Boyle] was speaking in the early stages about the entire ceremony, I felt I had to strip away and simplify stuff because everything was so spectacular and powerful, and I couldn't match that. In that sense, I was being quite Japanese, in the sense that I wanted to empty the space rather than fill it because I felt they needed an opposition to what was happening.'

That simplicity continued as the dance segued into Emeli's rendition of 'Abide With Me', as she took up the heartbeat that Khan's troop had danced to and used it as the introduction to the song. 'We wanted to do "Abide With Me" but we wanted people to hear it again properly and listen to it,' director Danny Boyle said in a commentary to accompany the DVD release of the Games. 'Because it is a song about mortality – it's obviously a religious song but if you're not religious it's still a song about mortality.'

'I don't think I'll ever have an audience that big ever again and to have that responsibility – that's what made me so nervous at the opening ceremony,' Emeli later recalled in an interview on Radio 2. 'I really wanted to learn about the song ["Abide With Me"] and know how it was written. I think having that knowledge and that pressure with me made me even more nervous. I don't think I'll ever be that nervous again but what a privilege. I don't think I'll ever feel that privileged to perform a song again.'

The use of the haunting hymn was a trick Boyle had utilised before, using the song in his zombie film *28 Days Later*. 'It felt like a wonderful place to do it because outside this stadium there are thousands of the fittest, most perfect specimens of humanity waiting to come in. We thought, before that we'll remind them that we all have a common fate. The guy who wrote this song wrote it three weeks before he died. He was in touch with death as he wrote it. Even if you don't believe in God – it's like that thing that Billy Connolly said: "I don't believe in God but I believe in people who do" – its value is indelible without you trying to narrow it by saying its religious. It's cultural and that's something we all carry.'

Afterwards, Emeli said: 'I will never forget tonight. Thank you so much to Danny Boyle and all his team for this incredible experience. I am extremely proud and humbled to be part of the amazing ceremony which will allow the world to see some of the best up-and-coming and established talent the UK has produced.'

Emeli's mum, dad and sister Lucy were all in the stadium for Emeli's performance. 'It was very surreal and as a mum you always worry that something is going to go wrong and I don't think we drew breath,' she told her hometown paper the *Piper* when asked about her daughter's performances and her career so far. 'It's all good, a bit like a rollercoaster with mainly ups. We have been going to her concerts for years helping out so we have seen it gradually build up. But this past year things have really taken off.'

Unfortunately, not everyone in the world got to see her performance. US broadcaster NBC opted out of the segment, instead running an interview with swimmer Michael Phelps carried out by *American Idol* host Ryan Seacrest.

Khan was oblivious to what had happened until a journalist told him at a press conference the following day. 'I am really sad that I couldn't show the work in America, and that really upsets me, because I don't think it's any less or more than any of the other pieces,' Khan told reporters. 'Is it not accessible enough? Is it not commercial enough? It brings to mind the question – but maybe I'm wrong because I don't really know the reason – but it brings to mind a question that maybe it's too truthful, and I think that says it all really.'

NBC's response was that they hadn't realised the segment was a tribute to the British 7/7 victims – almost making the matter worse by suggesting it wasn't aired because the section wasn't about

America. 'Our program is tailored for the US television audience,' said NBC Sports spokesman Greg Hughes. 'It's a credit to Danny Boyle that it required so little editing.' There were others affected by the NBC cull – the Arctic Monkeys were cut short as were sections featuring the Sex Pistols and Britpop bands. In some ways, the row could be said to have benefited both Sandé and Khan; afterwards the internet and social media kicked in, pushing people towards online versions of the performance and causing #NBCfail to start trending.

In the UK an estimated 27 million people watched the ceremony – the worldwide audience is believed to have been in the region of a billion. With or without NBC, it was a mind-boggling platform for any singer to appear on. 'When you're involved in something that big, you just don't know how people are going to respond,' Emeli later told the BBC. 'You could feel everyone was nervous about what the press was going to think, and how it would be perceived. So the reaction was wonderful. I was ecstatic the performance went well… and that I didn't fall over! I've watched it back once and it feels like, oh, is that me? It's such a surreal thing to see yourself perform in front of billions of people.'

Not everyone was impressed by Boyle's vision: just as Emeli was finishing her song and the competitors began to enter the stadium – The Parade of Nations –

British Conservative MP Aidan Burley tweeted: 'Thank God the athletes have arrived! Now we can move on from leftie multi-cultural crap.'

If there was any consolation to be had, it wasn't via Emeli's pay packet. Though the professional dancers and featured actors were all paid the going rate, musical performers – including Sir Paul McCartney, who ended the show with a 'Hey Jude' sing-along – received a token amount for their efforts. 'I got paid £1 for my work,' Emeli told the *Daily Telegraph*. 'It's there in print and I know because I signed the contract myself. Mind you, I haven't received anything yet! When I do, though, that £1 will be truly special. Part of what made the whole event so special was the volunteers who were paid nothing and even paid for their own accommodation. It shows how important art is.'

But the reward for many of the performers – Emeli included – would come in a different way as the Olympic effect kicked in on record sales for those artists whose music featured in the ceremony. The music industry's trade body, the BPI, reported that 50 songs used in the opening ceremony had received a sales boost of nearly 200 per cent and that some songs' sales had even increased by more than 1700 per cent. The *Guardian* reported that as a result of the show, 'initial sales indications from the mid-week charts show that five of the songs featured in the opening ceremony are on course to make it into the Top 40 Official Singles Chart this weekend, including the Arctic Monkeys' cover of the Beatles track "Come Together", Emeli Sandé's version of "Abide With Me", and "Caliban's Dream" by Underworld which is currently in the Top 5.'

If the opening ceremony provided a lift for record sales, then the Games themselves delivered a feel-good boost to the nation. The doom-mongers were proved wrong and as the Olympics neared the finishing line it was time for Emeli to step up and perform one more time for the closing ceremony. The creative director of the closing show, Kim Gavin, promised an extravaganza involving 'our most globally successful musicians' and future musical talent. 'Music has been Britain's strongest cultural export of the last 50 years and we intend to produce an Olympic closing ceremony that will be a unique promotion of great British popular music,' he told the *Daily Mail*. 'For the closing ceremony, which will be titled "A Symphony Of British Music", we will not only be working with our most globally successful musicians, but we also want to use this opportunity to showcase our stars of tomorrow.'

Emeli had been the last act to appear before the athletes entered the stadium at the opening show – now she would be the first artist to perform at the closing show. On a newspaper-covered truck next to a newspaper-covered upright piano, she performed a short version of 'Read All About It Pt III', hardly the cleverest piece of staging ever seen. As the song came to an end she swiftly had to steady herself as the truck pulled away and the full, street party-themed show got underway.

There couldn't have been many flat-bed trucks to spare in London that night as a variety of acts were hoisted on board various lorries and then driven around the stadium. It seemed to mark a tone for the whole show – no one involved looked entirely comfortable. Madness barked their way through 'Our House', One Direction gave 'You Don't Know You're Beautiful' the back-of-a-lorry treatment and a host of supermodels posed along to David Bowie's 'Fashion' in a Bowie-themed section that contained no actual David Bowie. Emeli reprised 'Read All About It' to a montage of tear-stained athletes conveying the 'joy and the despair' of the previous fortnight. Elsewhere, the show was propped up by the old guard: a shaky George Michael played 'Freedom' and – outrageously – his new single 'White Light', and Annie Lennox, Queen and The Who did their bit to make sure the more mature audience was catered for.

Emeli would contribute one more time to the whole Olympic experience. At the end of all the bombast, a montage of suitably inspirational images and moments – so beloved by BBC producers – was cut to her version of John Lennon's 'Imagine'. It's not the easiest of songs to cover at the best of times – in front of a worldwide audience it was a big ask. Emeli had a pretty succinct description of being asked to cover such an iconic song: 'Pretty intimidating!' she told the I Love Manchester website. 'I remember when the BBC asked me to do it with the Olympics and at first I was very intimidated because it's one of the best-written songs ever, by such a legend. I loved being able to do my own interpretation and also introducing the song to a younger generation. I feel very honoured to be asked but also it's quite a scary thing to do.'

'In terms of what Britain has given to the world, music is a massive part of that,' BBC Sport's Jonny Bramley said. 'Throughout the Games we considered very carefully the music we used, choosing to reflect British artists and artists from the opening ceremony in our daily montages. For the end of the Games, we wanted a piece of music of epic proportions by an iconic British artist – and "Imagine" fits that brief perfectly. The lyrics sum up the emotions we have all experienced over the last few weeks and it bookends the Games brilliantly – we opened with Paul McCartney and we close with John Lennon. But we wanted a modern take on it so we asked one of the young British performers from the opening ceremony, Emeli Sandé, to record a new version. So it is a melding of a classic piece of music with an inspiring young British musician.'

It said a great deal about the closing show that the Sandé montage and the Spice Girls were particular highlights. The closing show was everything that Danny Boyle's opening effort wasn't: it was a perfunctory trot through the decades that lacked the wow factor and the big names that the opening show delivered. The critics, who had loved Boyle's show, weren't quite so impressed this time around. 'After her turn at the Opening Ceremony Emile Sandé returned twice with some *X Factor* tear-jerking balladry,' said the *Daily Telegraph*. '"Read All About It" was mawkish but the words were perfectly in tune with the mood of the nation.'

The *LA Times* said: 'For sheer Vegas ridiculousness, the closing ceremony's creative director and choreographer, Kim Gavin, may deserve a high-five, but the chaos of unchecked spectacle, coupled with a dartboard's worth of British B-listers and a few bankable exports (Muse, George Michael, Jessie J) does not a medal earn. Stretching to nearly three hours in the live-stream version I watched, Gavin did little to showcase a musical culture at its Olympian peak.'

NME.com went one step further, suggesting that the artists at the closing ceremony were purely there for their own gain. 'Another outing for Emeli Sandé,' the review said. 'In the opening ceremony she performed too but it wasn't so much about her then, as what she was singing: The Meaning had little to do with her domestic fame or career path. This time it was the opposite: entirely about Sandé as a PR-machined product – and she went on for ages. I have to believe both Adele and Leona turned down Gavin, for Emeli to have got this length of slot; I've forgotten anything about the song except the totally Adele-ish solo piano accompaniment.'

Regardless of the reviews, Emeli said she had 'loved every minute of the Closing Ceremony on Sunday.' She posted the following message on her Facebook page: 'So amazing to get to be a part of it all again and to see those wonderful performances from Jessie J, Tinie Tempah, the Spice Girls, Annie Lennox up close!! Felt proud to be British. Thanks to the organisers and to all of you for your lovely messages.'

The Games had an astonishing effect on the UK in many different ways. It was claimed the event would pull Britain out of recession and it was even credited with people being nice to each other in London. That didn't last long. But like many artists involved, the Olympics had a major effect on Emeli's success too – just days after the closing ceremony ended, *Our Version of Events* returned to the top of the charts. Martin Talbot of the Official Charts Company said: 'At a time when it is as hard as ever for new artists to break through, it is fantastic Emeli now has the official biggest selling album of 2012 so far.'

It was a massive event in what was proving to be a

big year – but an even bigger event was just around the corner. However, only Emeli and those closest to her knew about it.

Nine

The Montenegrin Daughter-in-Law

On Thursday 13 September 2012, Emeli was booked to appear at a nightclub in the coastal town of Kotor in Montenegro – or as the Montenegro Travel website put it: 'One of the leading British pop stars Emeli Sandé will perform in a discotheque "Maximus" on Thursday. Participant of the opening and closing ceremony of the Olympic Games in London impressed the world with lyrics of the songs she writes herself, the way she interprets them, and became a true star and pride of the British nation.'

Introducing herself with a little of the local language – which went down very well – she performed with just a guitarist and keyboard player.

The rather rowdy crowd sang along to every word in English. But it soon became apparent that there was more to the trip than simply a gig at the discotheque Maximus. Just before the show, Emeli's dad Joel was reported to have written on Twitter: 'Just about to embark on a 4hrs flight to hand my older daughter's hand in marriage. Feels surreal but great. Here's hoping everything goes to plan.'

Emeli and Adam had got married in secret in his native Montenegro. It took everyone by surprise, especially the press. The media preferred their pop stars to be a little more malleable, sell the story and the wedding photos to the highest bidder, and make sure everyone in the world knows about it. Not Emeli and Adam. A 'source' close to the family told the *Daily Record* newspaper: 'It was a fairly traditional service in the evening. Emeli looked beautiful in a designer dress. Her fiancé wore a lounge suit. There will be more celebrations before everyone heads home but Emeli now has some time off so will get to enjoy a proper honeymoon.'

Perhaps as an act of politeness to the country that hosted her wedding, Emeli did give one interview to Montenegro TV, which made the news the following evening. 'I wanted to do the traditional thing,' she said, confirming she was about to get married and that she planned to take Adam Gouraguine's surname. 'I want to be part of his life and his family, so I want to add his surname. I want to be part of his tradition. I grew up in a family of two different cultural backgrounds, so I embraced both. One day when we have kids, I'd like them to be the part of these two different cultures.'

When news of events in Montenegro began to filter out, Emeli's team released a statement that was terse to the point of being unpleasantly blunt. Adam was not mentioned by name and there was a slightly threatening undercurrent aimed at any media organisations showing undue interest in the story: 'We can confirm the fact that Emeli married at the weekend,' the statement read. 'But it is purely a private affair and no further details, quotes or pictures will be released, and we ask that her privacy is respected.'

Joel Sandé took a little of the tension out of the situation: 'It's been a great rollercoaster year to date and this can only make my baby's dream a more realistic version of her events,' he told the Scottish press. Nice quote, well put and he even got a subliminal plug for her album in. Perhaps those around Emeli could learn something from her dad.

It later transpired that Emeli's involvement in the wedding arrangements was zero. Her husband had done the lot. 'I gave it to Adam,' she later told the *London Evening Standard*. 'He did everything. Literally. When I got there he was like, oh yeah, let me show you the venue. It wasn't a church – it was just a place by the coast. And it was perfect. We got married at night and had a little honeymoon in Serbia. It was wonderful. A few Scots came from Glasgow. My friend Sam wore his kilt. He has such a strong Glaswegian accent, all the Montenegrins were like, we thought we could understand English until he turned up.'

Thanks to her marriage to Adam, Emeli earned herself a nickname in the Balkans: the Montenegrin Daughter-in-Law. Although she would go to great lengths to keep Adam out of the limelight – at one stage she refused to even confirm his name during interviews – Emeli was unapologetic about getting married at a relatively young age: 'It's really great being married,' she later told the *Sun*. 'We've been together for so long so it just felt like the natural next step. It feels fantastic – you have security and commitment. It's nice to have the stability and go home and know that's your man. Whatever happens he's got my back and I've got his.'

Back home in Hackney, it was back to business. Rihanna had decided to include 'Half of Me' – a song Emeli had been involved with – on the 'deluxe' edition of her new album *Unapologetic*, a huge coup as the release was sure to hit No 1 on charts around the world. 'I sent songs to [songwriting and production team] Stargate in New York who work with Rihanna and they asked me to finish the song for her. I met her in LA and she told me how much the song meant to her. It was great to hear that there was an emotional connection. She said, "I don't know what you have been through but you are a poet and this song has really moved me." Hearing that from Rihanna was pretty amazing. It moved her a lot because it is about what you see of Rihanna on TV being half of who she is. There is a lot more you don't understand. Lyrically, I'm proud of the song and can't wait to hear what she has done with it. I haven't heard it yet. I'm going to have to go buy it to hear it.'

After a summer of Sandé success, a new version of *Our Version of Events* was released with additional tracks. The album now continued with 'Wonder', a carnival-themed track that Naughty Boy would release as a single with Emeli as the featured singer and that was also due to form part of his debut album, *Hotel Cabana*. 'I hadn't made a beat like "Wonder" before and I was just thinking, how can you get the energy of a dance tune but without having to actually make that kind of music and still keep it organic?' he told *Sound on Sound*. 'I was just experimenting with that idea with the drums, purely layered loads of sound, and it just seemed to work. And there's no real snare on "Wonder" as well, because every time I put a snare on it, it just started sounding like a dance beat. It was definitely Bollywood-inspired, because they love their big epic kind of drums. I wanted "Wonder" to have that balance of commerciality but not be cheesy – do you know what I mean? I still like keeping my edge as a producer because I do want people to think they get something different with me but, obviously, I still want to make commercial music for the most amount of people. It's probably the happiest track I've made.'

Emeli travelled to a flooded forest in Denmark to film the video for 'Wonder' with Naughty Boy and Danish director Nadia Marquard Otzen. She learned how to handle a small motorboat to cross a smoke-shrouded lake – with two blonde Danish lifeguards watching her every move – as painted dancers gyrated around a pink-tinged forest. It wasn't an easy task to turn the forest that colour, as director Otzen explained to Promo News: 'As a director you can sometimes be met with a bit of eye-rolling at your ambitious ideas and I was kind of expecting that when asking to turn all the greens in a forest from green to pink.'

Despite the fact that the song was essentially his single, Naughty Boy kept a typically low profile in the video – it's the back of his head wreathed in smoke in the opening shot and the remaining glimpses of him are so brief that even his mum might struggle to spot him. The focus is firmly on Sandé.

As a single, the track got to No 10 in the UK charts. It also gained a fresh lease of life as the soundtrack to an advert for Littlewoods featuring Myleene Klass. As an album track, it gave the new version of *Our Version of Events* a kick-start at the point where it had previously finished. The next track on the new version was an alternative, more urgent take on 'Breaking the Law'. Compared to the airy, low-key original version, this one had a drive and push with drums and cellos egging the song on. It's uplifting and affirming compared to the original – but it's not as good.

'Easier in Bed' – co-written with Chris Loco who'd worked with Rita Ora and Leona Lewis – is next. It had been around in demo form on Emeli's MySpace page for some time. It's sonically and lyrically the most unusual thing on offer on either version of the album with its clicks, clocks, synth washes and throbs. It's a rather out-of-character Sandé tale of a relationship that has no meaning beyond the physical. The whole effect is disorienting and uneasy – just like the protagonists in the song – and it's rather wonderful.

Next is the duet 'Beneath Your Beautiful', another track that would have a life outside of *Our Version of Events*. It also featured on the debut album by Labrinth, otherwise known as producer and songwriter Timothy McKenzie. He'd been signed by confirmed Sandé fan Simon Cowell to his Syco Music label, normally the home for acts culled from his TV talent shows. Labrinth had already made an uncredited appearance on a No 1 single with Tinie

Tempah's 'Pass Out'. With Emeli Sandé and 'Beneath Your Beautiful' he got to the top of the charts again, but this time everyone knew it was him. 'That song relates to everyone,' Labrinth later told the IamMusic.TV channel. 'We're all little kids inside, faking it. I like the sentiment of the song, we've all been there. You've got to take all the crap away and get to the real person underneath. That's what the song is about.' The song also managed to annoy fans of grammar too, believing it should be called 'Beneath You're Beautiful'. 'I love how crazy this has sent people,' Labrinth wrote on Twitter. 'It was to annoy English teachers and grammar Nazis.'

Emeli had known Labrinth for several years, when both were struggling to get their first breaks. 'I first worked with him two years ago, before I was signed and before he was signed as well,' Emeli told the Arjan Writes website. 'He was very different and I could tell that straight away. He's a musician more than anything else. I loved working with him. We got really nerdy about music and talking about all the theories of music. You can't really do that with many people in the industry. I have a lot of respect for him. To have the chance to work with him and to be on his album is fantastic.'

The song had originally been written for US singer-songwriter Mike Posner, who's worked with Justin Bieber. Posner has a writing credit on 'Beneath Your

Beautiful', but insisted that Labrinth take the song on board: 'It was originally started by me and Mike Posner,' Labrinth said. 'He was so passionate in the studio, he was like, "Bro, I don't understand. They don't see who you are, Lab! You're a rock star! They need to see what you do." When we started working on the song it was initially written for him. I sang the demo, but he suggested to record the song myself. That was really cool and eventually when the song was created, we thought that Emeli would be perfect to duet with on the record. She came to the studio and she ended up writing her whole own verse, and created her own interpretation of what the song is about.'

The video to accompany the song's release as a single featured giant-sized images of each artist projected onto what's believed to be the largest rear projection screen in the UK. It was directed by video industry veteran Sophie Muller, who had made promos for everyone from Blur to Gary Barlow. It was a widescreen video for a widescreen song.

Finally on the new version of *Our Version of Events* is the version of John Lennon's 'Imagine' recorded for the BBC to use for the outro montage of the Olympics. Is it a well-rendered and perfectly respectable version of the song? Yes it is. Did the world really need another version? Probably not. But that didn't stop the new edition taking *Our Version of Events*' overall sales to triple platinum status. 'O.V.O.E = TRIPLE PLATINUM!!!! Thank you all!!!' Emeli posted online.

When the awards season kicked in Emeli seemed to be everywhere at once, normally walking out with some kind of trophy. She was named Musician of the Year at the *Harper's Bazaar* Women of the Year Awards. It was also announced that she was up for five MOBO Awards and she won three of them: Best Female, Best R&B/Soul Act and Best Album. 'I really didn't expect to get three,' she said at the ceremony in Liverpool. 'I feel fantastic, I feel like all the hard work pays off when you get acknowledgement like this, so I'm very happy.' She also got to meet rapper Wiley for the first time. Despite sharing a major hit with 'Never Be Your Woman', they'd never been in the same room before.

She also won Best Solo Artist at the prestigious Q Awards at the Grosvenor Hotel in London. 'Wonderful!' she told *Viva* magazine. 'I was there last year and was nominated for Best New Artist, so it's great to come back and win it a year later. I just felt great and I didn't think I would win it considering who I was up against, so to get that acknowledgment was fantastic.'

She even won the James Joyce Award from the Literary and Historical Society of University College Dublin. She joined an eclectic mix of previous recipients, including author Salman Rushdie, Harry Potter creator J.K. Rowling and White Stripes frontman Jack White. 'All her many successes as a songwriter, as a solo artist with a debut album that is nothing short of stunning, and indeed the very qualities she embodies, tell of a star fast on the rise, and saw her inexorably most deserving of this award,' gushed Daisy Onubogu of the UCD Literary and Historical Society.

It seemed like Emeli was omnipresent – award ceremonies, the Olympics, the premiere of the Bond movie *Skyfall* – and some commentators began to flag up the danger of her becoming overexposed. It was a suggestion that seemed to provoke an uncharacteristically angry response from the singer. 'I feel like it's a bit unfair,' Sandé told the *Sun*. 'I actually haven't done that much, but it's just what I have done have been huge events. If I was at the MOBOs, it was because I was nominated, or if I performed at something, it's because I was asked. It's not like I was forcing myself on anyone. Everyone is entitled to their own opinion, but I worked so hard to get any exposure at all, so I don't see that as a negative. People who were critical of that weren't there when you're working your arse off trying to get a record, and when you're trying to get someone to listen. They don't know how that feels. So I take it as a positive. It's all about getting your music out there, and who knows, I might not get that kind of exposure next year, or ever. I'm happy.'

Meanwhile a bold plan hatched the previous year by her management was coming together. It would take the kind of venues Emeli played to another level. 'Last year I was hoping that we would be able to play the Royal Albert Hall by the end of this year,' Emeli's manager Adrian Sykes told *Sound on Sound*. 'And we are doing that. You have to have the ambition.' Ambition? Even before the show had taken place it was announced that it would be filmed and released as a DVD and CD.

The emphasis for the show – performed on 11 November – was spectacle, drama and above all... class. Cameras swooped through the highest levels of the 19th-century building, more usually used for classical concerts. In recent years a certain sense of having 'arrived' was conferred on pop acts playing there, indicated by Sandé's comment at the start of the show: 'Wow! I'm playing the Royal Albert Hall!'

Dressed all in black, shrouded in blue lights and backed by a flotilla of backing singers and a string section, the show opened with 'Daddy', given a church-like, ethereal quality that seemed to fit the surroundings.

Emeli took to the piano for 'Clown' and a cover of 'I Wish I Knew How It Would Feel to Be Free'. Nina Simone's version is generally regarded as the definitive take on the song and Emeli acknowledged her heroine in the song's introduction.

Then, just as 'Read All About It Pt III' was turning into a cosy ballad, Professor Green appeared – all tattoos and T-shirt – and dragged the song back to its original version. This was the point that the Albert Hall crowd got on their feet, whipped out their mobiles and start treating it like a gig instead of a recital. Emeli managed a quick costume change into a little red dress for 'Wonder'. The real show seemed to have kicked in thanks to the good Professor: the seats, for which the audience had paid handsomely, were now largely unused.

There were more hits in the shape of 'Mountains' and 'Heaven' before Labrinth made an encore appearance for 'Beneath Your Beautiful'. The final song, 'Next to Me', was dedicated by Sandé to 'my brand new husband'. As the show ended and Emeli soaked up the applause, she waved to the upper tiers of the Hall. There was her family, including her new husband Adam Gouraguine. One figure stood taller than the rest – her father Joel Sandé. He was doing what he had done at every one of his daughter's performances – he was recording the show with his ever-present video camera.

'Huge MASSIVE thank you to Professor Green and Labrinth for joining me on stage last night and making it such an epic night!!!' she posted on her Facebook page the day after the show.

If it seemed audacious for such a new artist to play

such a prestigious venue, then that's probably because it was. No one seemed more acutely aware of this than Sandé herself: 'Two years ago I opened for Alicia Keys and I remember stepping out and thinking, whoa, imagine if you could sell this place out yourself... and I thought maybe in five or six years it would be possible,' she later said in a BBC interview. 'So that was a really great night, a real summary of how the year had gone. My whole family was there and my friends had come down from Scotland – but the party on stage was probably better than the after-party! After the adrenalin goes down, you just want to go home. But I remember really enjoying being on stage, and that's not something you can guarantee every night.'

As far as the Albert Hall crowd were concerned, Emeli could do no wrong that night. They applauded and whooped her every word and mouthed along to every song. But some reviewers pointed out that the venue, the show and the way it was presented made one thing very clear: the clubland hitmaker of 'Funky Drummer' samples and urban sensibilities seen in her debut 'Heaven' had changed. 'Her performance confirmed what we already knew: she has a remarkable voice, plenty of songwriting talent, some rousing, direct pop songs – and a weakness for pushing the schmaltzy button a bit too often,' said the *Daily Telegraph* in its review. 'While most of Sandé's upbeat songs veer well clear of falling into the asinine pop trap, the same can't be said for her ballads. She couldn't resist a long, dreary segment of the mushy stuff, backed by twinkly percussion and string sections. The crowd – which ranged from families to trendy twenty-somethings, a mark of the ubiquity she has achieved this year – was mercifully woken up when rapper Professor Green appeared to give "Read All About It" a smouldering crescendo, his cheeky bravado delivering some welcome oomph.'

'At times during her more passionate display,' said the Entertainmentwise website, 'she was reminiscent of a preacher as she paced the stage shouting every word with conviction – perhaps with the hope that someone in the audience's life could change by her words.'

'Sandé has performed on some huge stages,' said Sarah Deacon on The Huffington Post website. 'Over the summer I saw her at Bestival and at the Olympics – but nowhere has suited her as perfectly as the Royal Albert Hall. A place made for huge voices like hers, yet intimate enough for fans to connect emotionally with every note.'

In December, Emeli sang 'Clown' at *The X Factor* final – the Simon Cowell-created boy band One Direction were also on the show. The following year, Emeli's advice to singers regarding appearing on shows like *The X Factor* would essentially be: don't do it. But that night, what she told finalists James

Arthur and Jahmene Douglas was this: 'I would say, enjoy it. You've gotten so far and tonight is just such a special night, everyone is here to show love, just have a good time.'

Among the judges on the show that night was Take That main man Gary Barlow, who'd turned down the chance of signing Emeli to his record label. If Emeli had any hard feelings, she didn't show them. The same couldn't be said for her musical collaborator Naughty Boy, who tore a strip off Barlow in an interview with the *Daily Record*. The memory of that rejection was clearly still very fresh in his mind: 'Between the two periods of time, she has not become a star,' he said. 'Because she was always a star. She performed "Clown" on *X Factor* at the final in December so it has all come full circle. I saw Gary Barlow there because I was with Emeli. He knows inside that he made a mistake. It's something that nobody else knows and, as he is a judge on *The X Factor*, he should be shamed for this. He is a great writer and singer, but I don't respect the fact that she is the biggest star of the year on *The X Factor* and he couldn't see it. It is about time that Barlow came out in the public domain, because spotting talent is a gift. One audition on *X Factor* and people are told they either are or aren't stars. Obviously, some people aren't. But there are others that should be given more of a chance and encouraged. He needs to man up. He has never even mentioned that he knew Emeli and turned her down. It's his guilty secret.'

Perhaps deeds were better than words. Two months after the *X Factor* appearance, Emeli announced that she was planning to start her own record label, to help performers avoid some of the problems she had experienced. 'When I was trying to get signed, when I was going for all these meetings and people were looking at me like, what do we do with you? I built a reputation as a songwriter before my own hits. People were coming to me for songs – I wanted to keep songs like "Clown" and "Mountains" to sing myself. But the record labels saw me as a songwriter. It was hard to get people to believe in me. I think I'm going to start a label – that's the business plan. That's what's happening.'

There would be further gigs – though none quite as upmarket as the Royal Albert Hall – in Glasgow, Birmingham and Canada as the year drew to a close, but there would be the opportunity for one more performance before Christmas in her home town. On 21 December, the last day of term, pupils at Alford Primary were gathered in the school hall to sing Christmas carols when head teacher Liz MacLeod told pupils they had a special visitor. In walked Emeli Sandé. 'I don't think I will ever forget the look of surprise, shock and excitement on such happy faces,' Liz MacLeod told the local paper, the *Deeside Piper*. 'This was probably the hardest secret I have ever had to keep! I knew there was a chance she would visit, but it was not confirmed until Thursday. None of the staff knew and so it was a total surprise for them too. Emeli spoke to the children and reminisced about sitting in assemblies in the same hall when she was a pupil in the school. She laughed at how it now looked so much smaller to her. She presented us with her framed award for selling a million copies of her album.'

Emeli sat at the school's piano and played 'Next to Me' and 'Clown', which had been confirmed as her new single. Liz MacLeod: 'It has certainly been a very special year for our very special ex-pupil. To think that she has performed at the Olympic Stadium and in the Royal Albert Hall, and yet was happy to return to sing in a little primary school shows just how grounded she is.' Emeli told BBC Scotland: 'My mum had managed to organise the surprise with the head teacher from my primary school and for the academy as well. So we went and surprised the kids. It was their last day of the term and they had just come back from their Christmas party and they weren't expecting it at all. We managed to keep it a secret from the teachers as well so it was really lovely.'

Two days later, *Our Version of Events* returned to the top of the charts. It was now a quadruple platinum album, with sales of 1.4 million: 'Christmas #1 album!' Emeli posted online. '2012 you have my heart x.'

It would be Emeli and Adam's first Christmas as a married couple, but they weren't going to spend it together. Emeli would be in Scotland and her husband was heading to Montenegro. 'I won't see him,' she confided to the *Sun*. 'But we'll be in Dubai for New Year because I'm doing a show there, so that will be nice. I try to go home every year for Christmas. Everything shuts down in the music industry at that time of year and I just get to go home – it's great to get back every year.'

Our Version of Events was now the officially the biggest selling album of the year – 'London Adele' was next with *21* and Ed Sheeran was third with +. Emeli was named iTunes Artist of the Year. Many reviewers put her in their Best of the Year lists and Adrian Thrills in the *Daily Mail* summed up the media's attitude towards Sandé's success: 'Just as Adele dominated 2011, a former medical student from Aberdeenshire towered imperiously over 2012. Emeli Sandé won a Brit, sang at the Olympics, stole *The X Factor* final and even gave away some of her best songs to Rihanna and Alicia Keys. With a debut characterised by expressive vocals and heart-wrenching lyrics, she also made my album of the year. In an era of manufactured idols, there is something reassuringly authentic about Sandé.'

It had been Emeli's year. 'A lot has been crammed into this year,' she told Clare Balding in an interview on Radio 2. 'From releasing a debut album which is something I'd dreamt of since I was seven, the Olympics, the tours – I got married in September – so I really don't know how I'm going to do more in 2013. It's a year I'm never going to forget.'

Ten

If I Don't Party Tonight... Then I'll Never Party

The New Year started with a new chart record: Emeli became the first solo artist to notch up 47 unbroken weeks in the Top 10 of the album charts. The company she was starting to keep in terms of success was daunting – no solo act had managed such a run before, but a band had. They'd managed a 62-week run with their debut – and that band was The Beatles with *Please, Please Me*.

Meanwhile the momentum was increased with the news that Emeli was leading the nominations for the 2013 Brit Awards: '3 Brit nominations!!!' she tweeted. '#BRITsnoms – to everyone that's been there since the Critics' Choice and years before that THANK YOU!!!'

Emeli had nominations for Best Female, Best Album and two songs in the running for Best Single, 'Next to Me' and the Labrinth collaboration 'Beneath Your Beautiful'. 'It's a really good feeling,' she told the BBC when the full list of the Brits nominations was released. 'It feels great, a bit scary, because you never know, you might not win anything. It's great to have this acknowledgement a year after winning the Critics' Choice award is really, really cool. The Brits is an institution and acknowledges music from all different genres, whether you're commercially successful or you're just a fantastic artist. I remember seeing [girl-group] Eternal [on the Brits] thinking, one day I'll be up there, so it's like a dream come true. I'm going to be a lot more nervous this time, but fingers crossed, positive thoughts, we'll see what happens.'

The possibility of stocking up her awards cabinet was the backdrop to Sandé's real assault on America as her month-long US tour got underway. This time she was taking husband Adam with her. 'He's going to come on tour,' she confirmed in an interview with Radio 2. 'He's doing his PhD at the moment so hopefully he can take his numbers and his facts with him. We're just going to try and work it out. He's very supportive.'

The tour started in Atlanta, hitting cities like Chicago, New York and San Francisco along the way before ending at the House of Blues in San Diego. 'It feels quite exciting to start from that grassroots level again,' she told *Rolling Stone* magazine. 'It's all about the fans and about that connection. I hope we can go from state to state and try and build it. People have heard of my name but that's about it. You still have to win everybody over, but that's the pressure which I work best under.'

Reviewers began to start building a case for Emeli's success in America as being almost inevitable. 'Sandé's one-hour set left little to be desired, but the highlights definitely included the subdued "Suitcase", which she performed accompanied only by her bassist, and the defiant "My Kind of Love",' said the MSN website, reviewing the New York show. 'She closed the show with "Next to Me", the debut single that first brought her attention, and proved to be her biggest stateside single to date. There are quite a few soulsters which have invaded the US shores over the last few years, and while she may not have the flash of some – Emeli Sandé definitely has the pipes to really plant roots in American soil.'

In an interview with music industry magazine *Billboard*, she explained the plans behind the US invasion. 'I think my biggest challenge for this year is bringing the music over here [North America] and to the rest of Europe,' she said. 'The way I'm approaching it is the same way we did in the UK. It's so important to build a fan base from the grass roots up and start with very small shows and a real emphasis on live music. That's what I'm doing here, just doing small shows and building naturally. You can't really force it, so I'm just trying to introduce the music slow and steady. I'm trying to write on the road, but I think I need to finish these tours and really sit down and dedicate some proper time to writing.'

She also said she'd like to relocate to America for a while to make the 'invasion' easier to mount, but denied she was thinking of leaving the UK altogether. 'Being able to do this tour now gives me a chance to scope out each city along the way. I really liked Atlanta. I really like New York. I'm sure I'll work in England some more, too. I'm just so happy the people in the UK could really connect to the music, and I'm not abandoning them or anything like that.'

Some big musical hitters in the States were also getting behind Sandé. Jay-Z was predicting big things for her. 'Emeli has the talent to be big in America, no doubt,' he told the *Daily Star*. 'She has a unique sound and she is going to be a big deal. There is a great tone to her voice. She is going to sell a lot of records. I read it's her dream to work with Bey [his wife Beyoncé] and all I can say is you never know. You have to be extraordinary to break into the US. If the talent is there, it can be done. Adele is proof of that.'

'London Adele' had just racked up three No 1 hits in America – 'Rolling in the Deep', 'Someone Like You' and 'Set Fire to the Rain' – and she was by now selling three times as many albums in the US than Lady Gaga. What's more, she was up for six awards in February's Grammys. She could do no wrong in most people's eyes. Only one issue seemed to niggle with some: her weight. Designer Karl Lagerfeld called her 'a little too fat' and comedienne Joan Rivers had said that Adele should rename one of her hits 'Rolling in the Deep Fried Chicken'. 'She's a chubby lady who's very, very rich,' Rivers said.

As the Grammy ceremony approached, Emeli – who was still in the States after her tour – also came under scrutiny about her weight, or lack of it. Commenting on her arrival at a pre-Grammys party hosted by US music legend Clive Davis, the *Daily Mail* said: 'Emeli Sandé was almost unrecognisable on Saturday night as she showed off the results of her dramatic weight loss on the red carpet at the pre-Grammy party at the Beverly Hilton in LA. Cutting a very different figure to the one she's known for, the 25-year-old made the most of her shrinking waistline in a tight black skirt and cream top. Clearly not planning on ditching her demure and sophisticated style just because she's lost some weight, the award-winning singer stuck to her usual edgy take on retro chic.'

As if to reinforce how she'd now become fodder for the gossip columnists, the *Mail* also managed to slip in a fresh rumour while flagging up her weight.

'Quashing rumours that she's pregnant, the "Read All About It" singer showed off her tiny waist in the figure-hugging skirt and added a simple gold chain which complemented the delicate neckline of her top. The singer kept her trademark bleach-blonde quiff and added a touch of lip gloss and shimmery powder to her much slimmer face.'

Away from the gossip, her presence at the Grammy show was more important in musical terms because of the endorsement of Emeli by Clive Davis – the man who had mentored Whitney Houston. 'Clive Davis asked me to come and perform tonight and I was like, wow, yes!' she told reporters as she arrived. 'Even in Scotland I've heard about the Clive Davis party, it's so legendary. So many people have performed here and debuted here. I'm so excited.'

As Emeli took to the stage of the pre-Grammy event, Davis described Emeli as 'the one to watch.' He told the audience that Emeli's performance was something they wouldn't forget in a hurry: 'She's about to break in a big way.' Emeli performed 'Heaven' and 'Next to Me' that night. 'What a night,' Emeli tweeted after the show.

As the US tour ended, Emeli's new single 'Clown' was released. The accompanying, slightly pretentious black-and-white video was shot at Black Island Studios in Acton, London. It saw Emeli, surrounded by jackbooted men, on trial for being artistically free and being asked to sign her life away. 'It's about how I felt when I was trying to get signed,' she said in publicity material to accompany the single's release. 'I was going for all these meetings and people were looking at me like "What do we do with you?" It's about not allowing yourself to be judged by others or to be taken for an idiot. I feel the video reflects that.'

Reviewers seemed to welcome the track with open arms. 'We really are all just waiting for Emeli Sandé to slip up and put a foot wrong, aren't we?' said music website UKMix. 'Even when singing on top of a milk float at the Olympics she seemed as poised and classy as ever. "Clown" is yet another checkmate for the Scottish singer, so it seems that we're going to have to wait just a little bit longer for that career-ending scandal. Lyrically "Clown" touches on Emeli's early struggles within the music industry; the difficulty of getting signed and the judgement that came with dreaded boardroom meetings. It's hard to believe that there were ever any artist development issues in the first place with this release serving as the closing chapter to such a flawless era. I guess the message of finding inner strength to overcome judgement that is embedded within the metaphors of "Clown" really is a testament to Emeli's success.'

The *Northern Echo*, the newspaper covering Emeli's North East birthplace, also approved: 'The latest single from the songstress's best-selling debut *Our Version of Events* is beautifully melodic and lyrically poignant. This self-affirming metaphor-laden masterpiece is about how Sandé felt when she was trying to get signed.'

Meanwhile, Scotland's *Daily Record* – always the most fervent of Sandé supporters – was also very much on-message: 'The biggest selling UK artist of 2012 releases a final tune to push those Christmas stocking sales of her album *Our Version of Events*. For me, "Clown" is one of the highlights of the album. It's big and deep and soulful. Just the usual for this great Scot.'

The single – backed again by acoustic track 'Kill the Boy' – reached No 4 in the UK charts, a good performance considering how long 'Clown' had been around.

Emeli Sandé Live at the Royal Albert Hall was released in February – the DVD/CD package from her gig the previous autumn. The reviews mirrored the kind of reaction Sandé tended to get from the press: ease off on the big ballads and the over-schmaltzy stuff, stay away from the middle of the road. The review on the BBC Music website summed that attitude up: 'Sadly, Sandé's live album has the same Achilles' heel as *Our Version of Events* – namely, too many accomplished but humdrum ballads... On the one hand, it feels mean-spirited to criticise Sandé's first live album. She gives a vocally impressive performance, backed by a well-drilled band, featuring all the songs fans would want from her. But only in her mid-20s, she's already looking like British pop's newest safe pair of hands:

the natural successor to Annie Lennox, though without the edgy earlier years.'

'The performance plays like a jubilant victory lap after Sandé's year atop the charts,' said the PopMatters website. 'There's plenty of corny banter with the audience about how they can achieve anything if they try. And everywhere there's Sandé's voice, strong enough to earn her this victory lap, and hopefully flexible and exciting enough to give her the opportunities for several more.' The *Daily Mail* said: 'As live albums go, it isn't perfect. Emeli has the soulful voice and songwriting abilities of [Nina] Simone, but she has yet to acquire the stagecraft that is a hallmark of her other great influence, Alicia Keys. While the New Yorker will fall back on her inner showgirl when she plays a big venue, the naturally reserved Sandé can seem overwhelmed by the occasion.'

The release paved the way for what would prove to be an early highlight of 2013 for the singer: the Brit Awards on 20 February at London's O2 Arena. The bookies had made her favourite in two categories: she was odds-on to get Best Album ahead of Mumford & Sons, Plan B, Alt-J and Paloma Faith, and the good money was on her to win Best British Female Solo Artist too, ahead of Amy Winehouse, Jessie Ware, Paloma Faith and Bat for Lashes. With four nominations in all, much was expected of Emeli that night. 'I don't know if I can win all of them,' she told

TV presenter Alexa Chung on the red carpet, 'but I hope I can win one.'

In fact, she won two. The Best British Female Solo Artist statuette was handed to Emeli by pop country singer Taylor Swift. 'Wow, this is amazing, this is incredible,' she said. 'I'm so happy to win this. I was up against so many wonderful artists. Thank you to my wonderful family, my mum, dad, my wonderful husband. Thank you to everyone who believed in me.'

When the winner of the Best Album category was read out by Roxy Music singer Bryan Ferry, it was Emeli who got to her feet. She hugged her husband Adam and producer Naughty Boy. 'This is a dream,' she said as she accepted the award. 'I think I'm a very unlikely pop star. You know this is an album I wrote because I didn't have the confidence to say these things in person. For me, so many people have connected with this album and found strength with these words, it makes me feel incredible and it doesn't make me feel as lonely. So, thank you everybody who bought this record. You make me feel as though I'm part of something much bigger. This is a dream really.'

As if to seal her place in the British music industry pecking order, Emeli had been chosen to close the show. Wearing a flowery Dolce and Gabbana dress, she started with 'Clown' at an upright piano before getting to her feet for a celebratory 'Next to Me', which got the full gospel choir and strings treatment.

Then the Brits were over for another year. Mum Diane and dad Joel were as ever, there, having their photo taken by the stage with their Brit programmes. 'Emeli worked so hard at this and she deserves it. She never gave up and it has paid off,' dad Joel told journalist Beverley Lyons. 'Perhaps if she had got this last year it would have been far too early, so it might not have worked out so well for her. We are both so happy for her.'

At the press conference after the ceremony, Emeli described her double win as a victory for the underdog. 'I was an underdog because I was a writer and nobody wanted to sign me,' she told journalists. 'Nobody thought I could sing my own songs. I think that's what gives me the edge. When people don't believe in you, you want to prove them wrong. I'd encourage any underdog to come and achieve their dreams and believe that anything is possible.'

Heading for an aftershow party on a boat moored just outside the O2, then on to the Hakkasan Hanway Place restaurant in central London, Emeli's tweet after the ceremony said it all: 'If I don't party tonight... then I'll never party #BritAwards2013'.

The following day, Emeli's success was the talk of Alford, especially at her old school. Moira Milne, head teacher of Alford Academy, told the *Daily Record*: 'Her successes last night and over the course of the last year are just reward for the incredibly hard work Emeli has put in over the years. We are all so proud of her. Everyone here at Alford Academy is speaking about her performance last night – she looked and sounded fabulous. There is a great buzz about the school. I know a few tears – happy tears – were shed by staff last night and pupils have said to me this morning, "Wow, she is such an inspiration to us. It's great to be an Alford pupil." She is a very talented lady and it is a privilege for us to have such close links with her. We all pass on our congratulations to Emeli.'

There was one more note of congratulation for Emeli – it came in the form of an email from a very prestigious fan via her husband: 'We got a message from the president of Montenegro,' she later told *Rolling Stone* magazine, 'which does quite stand out.' Another stand out was the effect that the double win had on Emeli's sales: six and a half million people watched the ceremony in the UK and a fair few of them clearly bought *Our Version of Events* after the Brits show had finished, as it went straight back to the top of the charts, with overall sales now passing 1.6 million in Britain. And for the first time, it sneaked into the Top 10 on the US iTunes chart.

In the run-up to the Brits, there was much talk of Emeli taking six months off, returning to Scotland and concentrating on writing. 'I'm happy to leave the limelight for a bit and lay low,' she told the *Sun*. 'I'm going to be in the studio working on my next album.

I just want to make more music, as that's my favourite thing.'

The chances of an extended break seemed unlikely though, because almost immediately after the dust had settled on the Brits, Emeli was in central London filming scenes for a new video on the London Underground before jumping on a plane back to America. She'd been asked to perform at Sir Elton John's annual AIDS Foundation Oscar party in West Hollywood Park, Los Angeles. 'Emeli Sandé's album, *Our Version of Events*, is a true work of art and a favourite of mine,' Sir Elton said in the run-up to her appearance. 'When she is on stage, you can feel her passion for music and the heart that goes into her lyrics. I can't wait to introduce Emeli to my guests and experience her live performance together. I predict that by next year she will be a multi-Grammy Award winner.'

Speaking about Sir Elton's invitation, Emeli told the BBC: 'He's been such a big supporter ever since the album came out. It's amazing to go out there – and I'll probably be singing with him as well. I have no idea what song... If I had to choose, "Rocket Man" would be cool. I can't wait.'

Among the crowd Emeli sang to at Sir Elton's party were Britney Spears, Miley Cyrus, Steven Tyler of Aerosmith and the Foo Fighters' Dave Grohl. 'I wouldn't have believed it last year, let alone when I was a kid,' she told *Rolling Stone* magazine after the show. 'You have to take a moment to let it all sink in and not move so fast that you don't realise what an insane night that was.'

That night she had shared a table with Bono of U2 and Emeli took the opportunity to pick the Irish singer's brains about cracking the US. 'We were sitting next to each other discussing the Oscars, and I was asking him questions about when U2 first came over to the States,' she says. 'It was really kind of crazy, now that I think about it. [Bono] talked about the first album – he was saying you tour, you keep plugging it. And Elton was the same. He was talking about how he was opening up for different people and all the little showcases they did here at the beginning. It was really encouraging and just cool to have their support.'

Back in Britain, Emeli started her UK tour in Birmingham. 'She kicked off the spine-tingling show with "Heaven",' said the Birmingham *Evening Mail*, 'walking on to an arena bathed in stunning white light which matched her sweep of platinum blonde hair. Her powerful but delicate voice ripped through the opening number, drawing a screeching cheer from the crowd at the end of the track which, somehow, managed to be louder than she when first walked out. Then it is into Sandé's world. One of carefully crafted meaningful lyrics about emotions and thoughts close to her heart, which she has turned into musical gold dust.'

Emeli swept through the UK's major cities and venues, including a three-night stand at London's Hammersmith Apollo. Posters for the tour proudly displayed the fact that every date had sold out. 'Had there been a 2013 Brit award for ubiquity, she would have bagged it too,' pointed out the *Guardian*. 'On her final night in London, night number nine of this UK tour, a year and a bit on from the release of her highly successful debut album, Sandé, though, retains all the vim of a debutant, despite two years of working this same material. As the night draws to a climax, "My Kind of Love" features a particularly powerful set of vocal lifts that stay on the right side of excess.'

The tour ended in a fitting place that in some ways brought Emeli's story full circle: Aberdeen. 'I'm coming home,' she tweeted before the two Aberdeen Music Hall shows. 'Final stop.'

The first Aberdeen gig had sold out in just over an hour when tickets had gone on sale. 'They flew out of the door at breathtaking speed,' said Joyce Summers from the venue. 'We knew it was going to be a hugely popular gig – Emeli obviously has an enormous following in a city which regards her with great affection as their own. People started queuing just after 7am and the phones have never stopped. Luckily we drafted extra staff in to cope with the calls, so all went well and we are now looking forward enormously to what is sure to be a fantastic gig on 19

April.' A second show was slotted in and that sold out even quicker: 'The tickets flew out of the door,' said Joyce Summers. 'And at 45 minutes, that's a new record for us, beating even Billy Connolly and Michael McIntyre.'

Impressive, but not a patch on the record that would tumble a few days later. On 28 April 2013 Emeli beat The Beatles' record for the number of consecutive weeks in the Top 10 for a debut album. They had managed 62 – Emeli racked up 63. A 50-year record that many thought was untouchable had been beaten. 'I'm completely lost for words and this is something I could only have dreamed of,' Emeli told OfficialCharts.com. 'The Beatles are the greatest band of all time and their legacy lives on and continues to inspire all of us that make music. I'm so happy that so many people have connected with the stories and the songs on the record; this really is our version of events now. I'd like to say thank you to everyone that has bought, played or shared my music in the last year: without your support this would never have been possible.'

Emeli's tweet when the news was announced summed up the enormity of the achievement: 'This record is so significant to me for many different reasons. I'm so happy and I'm thankful to you all. We made history!! #OVOE.'

★ ★ ★

That six months off seemed to be receding further into the distance. If anything, Emeli was even more visible. It was revealed that she'd reunited with the man behind the Olympic opening ceremony Danny Boyle, as he returned to his day job as a film director. Boyle had started the film – called *Trance* – before the Olympics and then picked up where he had left off when the opening ceremony was done with. Regular Boyle collaborator Rick Smith of dance group Underworld composed the soundtrack with contributions and additional tracks by Moby and UNKLE. Emeli's track, co-written with Smith, was 'Here it Comes', an upbeat piece with synth washes and a rhythmic vocal slightly reminiscent of 'Tonight' by American band Fun. 'It was wonderful to work with Rick again after the amazing time I had with him putting together the track for the Opening Ceremony at the Olympics,' Emeli said when the soundtrack and the film were released in March. 'I was honoured to be asked to collaborate with him again for the film and, with his help, I believe we have created something very special.'

Rick Smith said: 'For a film composer, working with Danny is a joy, because he's both a great collaborator and a giver of artistic freedom. He loves to be surprised, and also wants his film music loud and with presence, almost like another character – for me this is creatively exciting and inspiring. And it was a real joy to work with Emeli again – her passionate soulful voice and wonderful lyrics are a perfect ingredient of the score.'

Meanwhile another soundtrack opportunity had come Emeli's way in the shape of *The Great Gatsby*. The film's director Baz Luhrmann had heard an album by the Bryan Ferry Orchestra called *The Jazz Age*, in which some of the Roxy Music front man's best known songs were reinterpreted in a jazzy 1920s style. He was asked to expand the idea and incorporate it into Luhrmann's film, an extravagant 3D adaptation of F. Scott Fitzgerald's novel about 1920s life among the millionaire set. Emeli's contribution was a bustling, flapper-style take on Beyoncé's 'Crazy in Love'. 'It's quite amusing to do something that's so contemporary and take it back into the '20s style,' Ferry said in a short documentary about the making of the soundtrack. 'Which obviously fits the mood and period of the film.'

Emeli: 'I was asked if I'd like to come and do a version by the producer of the album. Bryan Ferry and his orchestra had put together this version. I was just honoured to be involved in the project and put my own spin on the song.'

Other artists to feature on the sound track included will.i.am, Lana Del Ray and Beyoncé herself. The soundtrack's executive producer was Jay-Z. No pressure on Emeli then as Mr Beyoncé was in charge of the musical side of the project. 'I tried not to think about it,' she told radio station 95.5 WPLJ. 'You'd probably go a bit mental if you were in the studio thinking about Beyoncé and Jay-Z... But I met him at the premiere and I think he liked it. He seemed really cool. I think because I did my own thing on it and it suited the film... it worked. He was standing next to Leonardo [DiCaprio] and Tobey Maguire, there were so many people around but I was like, I want to speak to Jay-Z. I want to know what he thought about the track.'

Reviews for the album were good – better than the film, in fact. 'Jay-Z executive-produced this score, which infuses F. Scott Fitzgerald's Jazz Age tale with the sounds of the hip-hop age,' said *Rolling Stone*. 'The result is an unusually diverting mixtape, with an all-star lineup: Beyoncé's "Crazy in Love" is here – in a jauntily jitterbugging cover version by the Bryan Ferry Orchestra, with vocals by British soul upstart Emeli Sandé.'

But as ever, critics can never agree when it comes to something Emeli's involved with. 'The songs, which meander in themes among partying, murder and heartache, mostly set their buttons on eerie and sad,' said The Huffington Post. 'The album is full of new cuts, previously released ones and covers. They all work, except for Emeli Sandé's strange version of Beyoncé's "Crazy in Love", which fails to combine modern sound with Charleston. It's more of a vaudevillian joke that falls flat.'

There was to be further Sandé soundtrack news when it was revealed that one of her songs was to appear in the TV show *Glee*. 'Next to Me' was performed in a straightforward, around the piano style by *Glee* regular Michelle Lea and *Wicked* Broadway star Idina Menzel in an episode called 'Sweet Dreams'. To celebrate, Emeli posted a picture of herself doing the *Glee* loser sign. The exposure on the show helped Emeli's original version of the track crack the US Billboard Top 50 for the first time, and boosted American sales of her album too.

Things were altogether more sombre in March as Emeli attended a memorial service to mark the 20th anniversary of the death of Stephen Lawrence, the black teenager who died after being stabbed in the street in a racist attack. Prime Minister David Cameron, Deputy Prime Minister Nick Clegg and London Mayor Boris Johnson were at the service at St Martin-in-the-Fields church in Trafalgar Square in London, alongside singer Beverley Knight, footballers Jermain Defoe and Sol Campbell, and members of the Lawrence family, including Stephen's mother Doreen. The service clearly had a great effect on the singer. Afterwards she took to the internet to quote Nobel Peace Prize winner and theologian Albert Schweitzer, known for missionary work in Africa and his writings on the life of Christ. 'In everyone's life, at some time, our inner fire goes out. It is then burst into flame by an encounter with another human being... We should all be thankful for those people who rekindle the inner spirit. #lawrencefamily.'

It also inspired her to start work on a new song that included a list of her heroes and heroines – Nelson Mandela, Nina Simone – with the working title of 'Drop it Low, Make it Rain'. She posted a swift clip of the 'song' online. It raised the question about new material from Emeli. The respected industry magazine *Music Week* had suggested that while it would have been quite easy for Sandé to tour *Our Version of Events* for the foreseeable future, it was believed that she was already working on new material. 'She's got to take some time to organise her thoughts and start writing songs for her next record,' a clearly very well-informed source told *Music Week*. 'It may happen quickly. It may take some time, but I think she would want another album to come out perhaps next year. She's very diligent and has a very solid work ethic. She's very serious about what she does, which is a joy.'

Meanwhile, the source claimed that Emeli's record label Universal, which now owns Virgin Records, would focus on making the singer's launch in the US a huge success. 'Since Steve Barnett has taken over at Capitol [Records] it's brought some real focus and order, and Universal love Emeli and they want it to be successful there.' There was also a great deal of confidence about Emeli's potential in the US: 'It's moving in the right direction. Her profile is building in the right way – they are feeling very confident they are going to have a successful campaign over there. While she's there we'll just book a studio somewhere for her to sit down and get her thoughts out.'

Emeli did indeed head to America and she posted the following message online to her fans: 'I'm going to be away for a while, the next step is New York and America. I know it's going to be hard work and a big challenge but I'm very excited about the journey ahead. I'm starting from scratch out there. Day one, square one.'

The initial plan involved appearing on high-profile shows like the *Dancing with the Stars*, Jay Leno's *Tonight* and playing a five-date tour in July, including three House of Blues gigs in Orlando, Houston and Dallas. 'I'm getting into my head how big the whole place is and how much work there is with the album,' she told industry magazine *Music Week*. 'I'm just getting used to the new [radio] formats and how everything works. It kind of reminds me of what it was like two or three years ago in the UK where a few fans who had heard about you turned up and you would see the audiences getting bigger and bigger.'

Her focus was so strongly on America that she didn't even return to Britain in May to receive the two prestigious songwriting awards she'd won. 'Woke up to the best news!!!!! 2 Ivor Novellos!!!!!,' she wrote on Twitter. 'Wish I could have been there, that would have been one excited speech!'

The reason why she wasn't able to attend and collect the awards for Best Song and Most Performed Work for 'Next to Me' was revealed by songwriter Anup Paul, who collected the awards on her behalf at a ceremony in London: 'I spoke to Emeli yesterday and she is just preparing herself for performing at the White House.'

Emeli had been invited to perform for President Barack Obama and a host of celebrities at the world's most famous address, for an event to honour US singer-songwriter Carole King. The 71-year-old was being awarded the Gershwin Prize for Popular Song, awarded by the US Library of Congress. King had set the template for female songwriters since the 1960s and her 1971 album *Tapestry* was a classic of the genre. Previous winners had included Paul Simon, Stevie Wonder, Paul McCartney and Burt Bacharach. 'Carole King will be the first woman to receive the Gershwin Prize for Popular Song from the Library of Congress,' Emeli posted online just before the event. 'I feel absolutely honoured to play a part in the celebration of her incredible musical legacy! The White House will be full of beautiful melody very soon!'

Watched by Obama and his wife Michelle, Emeli

sang King's classic '(You Make Me Feel Like) A Natural Woman'. Emeli also joined Gloria Estefan and country singer Trisha Yearwood to sing King's 1960s gem 'Will You Love Me Tomorrow'. President Obama pointed out to the audience that King had managed to write her first No 1 record when she was just 18. 'At this point, all of you are feeling like underachievers,' he joked.

'I wish I could put tonight in words,' Emeli wrote on Twitter after the show, trying to put into words the enormity of what had happened to her – not just that night at the White House, but over the last few years. 'It was just ...'

The girl from Alford had come a long way. One of her longest-standing supporters, DJ David Craig, summed it up succinctly in the space of one short tweet. Remembering one of her earliest gigs he wrote: 'From the Lemon Tree in Aberdeen to the White House #EmeliSande.'

Eleven

Music For Grannies?

The plan to break Emeli in America seemed to be going entirely to plan, if the message she tweeted on 11 June 2013 was anything to go by: 'Next To Me Goes Platinum in America!!!! #1MillBaby#slowlybutsurely.'

Her success in the UK doesn't seem to have happened 'slowly but surely' – it sometimes feels like she arrived fully formed. As we've seen, it didn't quite happen like that, but the question remains: why? Emeli Sandé is not as sexy as Rita Ora, she's not as edgy as Amy Winehouse, nor is she as fashionable as Florence Welch of Florence + the Machine. She occupies a position that is largely her own – she's not so much the British Beyoncé as the Scottish Alicia

Keys. She is the 'very unlikely pop star' – as she described herself while picking up two Brit awards. She's Scottish, she's mixed race, she writes, she performs, she's modest, she's married, she's a woman and she keeps her clothes on. There isn't anyone else like her – which means the music industry is likely to start demanding more people like her very soon. Expect a slew of Sandé clones any time now.

She has, in her own words, helped 'change what people's perceptions of what a pop musician should be. Maybe five years ago a pop musician would have making songs that weren't that... personal or too lyrical. I think people like Ed Sheeran, Adele, Amy [Winehouse]. Everyone who's changed what you have to do and what you have to be in order to be successful in the business.'

Then there's 'London Adele' – whether Sandé will ever equal the success of the young woman who shares her first name is highly debatable. But she's getting there: in the 2013 rich list of musicians under the age of 30, Adele topped the rankings with estimated earnings of £30m. Other names on the list include Jessie J (£8m), Leona Lewis (£12m) and One Direction (£5m each). Emeli went from nowhere to No 15 on the list. The other new entry on the chart was Ed Sheeran. The comparisons between the two Adeles are as inevitable as they're long-standing – despite the fact that Emeli changed her name to try to avoid them. As long as there are journalists asking Emeli questions, the question of what she thinks of being compared to Adele will always arise. 'It's great,' she told the *Daily Record*. 'I am a big fan of hers. We are very different lyrically. It's flattering to be compared to her because she is really good. She stands out because her lyrics are so honest and a lot of people can relate to them.'

The record-breaking album sales, the Olympics, the Brits, the Novellos, the Oscar parties, the White House – it seems like everyone loves Emeli Sandé. Well, nearly everyone. 'You look at the "best" now,' ex-Oasis leader Noel Gallagher told *Shortlist* magazine. 'Emeli Sandé? That is fucking music for grannies. I don't get it.' Emeli's response was somewhat uncharacteristic: she posted a picture of a granny giving the middle finger with the caption 'Thanks Noel'. Noel's brother Liam, now with his own band Beady Eye, came out in support of Sandé – well, what he actually said was: 'I like Emeli fucking Sandé. I think she's cool, man.'

Although it's not that difficult to get divided opinions in the Gallagher family, it does highlight the fact that Sandé divides opinion – some think Emeli and her music are cool, some think it's music that's a little safe – music for grannies. Perhaps the people involved in Sandé's story can help Noel 'get it'. The names of many of those interviewed for this book can be found in the 'thank you' section of *Our Version of*

Events – perhaps they can shed some light as to how Emeli Sandé has gone from medical student to megastar in such a short space of time?

'She's authentic,' says John Ansdell, the man who put up the money to release *Have You Heard?* – the 'lost' album from Emeli's Glasgow days. 'She's the complete artist. When I first came across her, she looked the part, had an amazing voice, a great songwriter, producer, musician. She had it all. The charts tend to be dominated by poppy, R&B, dancey tracks, maybe a few bands in there. But she's a real artist and I'd like to think that's the reason. She's written for quite a lot of artists too, which has raised her profile. Then there are the collaborations. The likes of the Olympics would have helped. Everybody of all ages loves her. Kids in primary school... she's their favourite artist. The grandparents who pick them up have her CD too. She appeals to everyone. She's got it.'

On *Our Version of Events*, John and his family are thanked for investing in Emeli's music. 'I didn't know at all,' John told me. 'I downloaded the album on iTunes and bought a CD about a week later. I had a wee nosey at the thank you page. It was quite nice – she thanked me and my family, which was a nice touch. I appreciated the mention. Quite a lot of time had passed. It was nice and my family appreciated it.'

John's label Souljawn is keeping the soul flame

burning, with releases by the late singer-songwriter Lynden David Hall as well as signing new acts like Sunshine Social and releasing their debut album. 'John is brilliant,' Emeli told the *Daily Record* when asked about the man who helped her in the early days. 'He is a really cool guy. He was a big supporter. He is great and his whole family are really lovely. It's brilliant to hear he is working on breaking new acts. I think he'll do very well.'

Urban Scot, the loose collective of DJs, producers and music fans that aimed to put Scottish urban music on the map were instrumental in spreading the word about Emeli at an early, grassroots level. Mel Awasi was a leading light with Urban Scot and now lives in Qatar. He says that of all the artists they worked with, Emeli was always the one to watch. 'In my career with Urban Scot I didn't meet anyone like Emeli,' he told me. 'I met a lot of amazing musicians and artists but with Emeli... she had a confidence. She knew her stuff. It was so natural for her. She's got a lot of substance. A lot of the stuff she's written... it isn't just bubblegum music. There's a story. Then there's her voice – it's not digitally manipulated. It's her. When you see her live it's the same. In fact, when you see her live it's better. Why her, why now? There's a gap in the market. Maybe if she'd come out a few years before maybe she wouldn't have been the success she is now – the demand wasn't there. Music is so diluted now – the production, the lyrics – I don't like the sounds we are currently producing. What she's done is come out with music that's appealing to all sorts of people and it's crossing different genres. Why now? I don't know. She's put a spell on us. She's a magician!'

DJ David Craig, another key player in Urban Scot, now lives and works at Nasimi Beach, at the Atlantis Palm resort, in Dubai – or as he puts it, 'just playing music in the sunshine.' He first spotted Emeli's potential when she was a teenager in Aberdeen and believes that the key to understanding her success is appreciating Emeli the songwriter. 'I remember asking her about writing songs,' he told me. 'How she could in one moment write a song for Susan Boyle and another write a song for Chipmunk? I asked her, how can you, as a young girl, understand the things you're writing about? I think her ability to do that is what defines her as an artist and what sets her apart from other people. Plus the fact she's always done it with an honesty and uniqueness. For every *X Factor* hopeful and auto-tuned bubblegum pop artist – there's been a bit of overkill in that department – here you have a girl who looks different, sounds different and actually brings a bit of honesty back into music.

'The record label deserves a lot of credit. It's not often these days that a label will be patient and nurture someone and develop them. I'm sure a decent budget went into promoting her as well. They really nurtured her and they were patient with her through her studies and they really developed her as an artist and I think that's the biggest, most telling factor in her success. The best thing they did with her was work on her as a songwriter before she released her stuff as a solo artist. Once she got that success as a songwriter it completed her as an artist. Now she's there, all she needs to do is continue to be herself and there's no reason why she can't maintain what she's got or even get bigger. The second album's always harder than the first one. She's set a standard for herself.'

David Craig's point that Emeli represents a breakaway from 'X Factor hopefuls and auto-tuned bubblegum pop artists' – and that the public can sense that separation – seems to have been adopted by Emeli herself. Though she has performed on both *The Voice* and *The X Factor*, Emeli has now seen fit to distance herself from the television talent show scene, despite the apparent admiration of Simon Cowell. 'I enjoy looking at the talent that's undiscovered and I enjoy watching the auditions,' she told Yahoo!omg!, 'but after that, it always makes me a little bit sad. It's a few people telling others whether they're good or not. Their confidence can be really knocked – it always makes me feel sad. I don't think *The Voice* is a natural representation of the music industry. I think it's false authority. I know how to be an artist in my own right, and what I love doing is writing. I don't think I'd ever have any right to tell anyone else whether they can make it or not. I don't think I'd feel comfortable in that position.'

She also weighed in with strong opinions about *The X Factor* too. 'I don't think I would have considered appearing on *The X Factor*,' she told the *Daily Star*. 'I would have been able to sing but I don't like the fact that nobody creates on the show. Writing needs to be encouraged. Finding an entry into the business isn't easy so I understand why people do it. You can tell when people want to be musicians or want to be famous. The kids who need music in their lives should just focus on their craft. I'd say don't be in a rush. The pressure they put on kids is for it to happen right now, but your talent will always be there.'

DJ Trevor Nelson was also someone who spotted Emeli's talent early on. He believes that it's her accessibility to so many different types of people that marks her out from other singers and helps explain her massive success. 'Emeli's career has gone beyond what anyone could imagine,' he told the *Daily Record*. 'She could have any career that she wants because she has got it on her own terms. I do seven shows a week across three BBC networks yet I can play Emeli Sandé on all of them. Musically, she has got that incredible range that transcends all ages.'

Nelson also cites 'London Adele' as being vital to

Sandé's rise, making it acceptable for a female singer to be understood and appreciated for what she was, rather than a record label's idea of what a young female singer should look like. 'Before Adele, what did people call a star?' he said. 'A girl in lingerie, who stands there in high heels. I personally think the music industry was leaning that way for a long time. I can honestly say that with the breakthrough of Adele it changed the attitude of a lot of the record labels because it is clear Emeli Sandé will not be hanging out at the opening of nightclubs. She is a class act and I think that makes her a star. She's a star purely on substance. Emeli is stripped down and old fashioned – "I'll write you a song and you'll get that song just through delivery" – and that is a star.'

The success and story of 'London Adele' is a constant theme through the story. To many people interviewed for this book, Emeli Sandé is still Adele, the girl from Alford near Aberdeen. To her family, she'll always be Adele. Well, nearly always. 'They call me Adele,' she told Radio 2 in 2012. 'Sometimes my sister calls me Emeli depending on her mood! But I feel I can really switch off and I still feel like Adele is still the med student in Glasgow and Emeli is the singer on tour.'

But these days, just how 'urban' is the one-time collaborator with the Urban Scot collective? She has gone from indie label, Neo Soul, piano diva to major label, Albert Hall conqueror with what almost feels like indecent haste. Where should she go from here? Is she lost now to the urban scene? Is she now too mainstream, too Radio 2 to reconnect with the same people who bought Wiley's 'Never Be Your Woman'? I spoke to Yasmin Evans, presenter on the BBC's urban station 1Xtra to find out if she believes Sandé can still engage with her original audience. 'I look at her and I see two different people,' Evans told me. 'From when I first saw her – she was this person who was "the girl's voice on a record". It was the Wiley collaboration, "Never Be Your Woman". I watched it back before I did this interview. I never realised it was her in the video as well. She had the curly hair. Then she came back with the short blonde hair – I didn't know it was the same person. Now she's one on a par with Adele. We are almost forced to play Emeli Sandé. I love her music, but some people are kind of rolling their eyes... oh this one again. Like Adele – it's reaching that level unfortunately. We've heard "Read All About It" parts one, two and three – now leave that alone!'

Perhaps it's no coincidence that in mid-2013, just as Sandé's mainstream success was reaching a high, her name was linked to slightly edgier projects. Electronic dance act Rudimental had seemingly come from nowhere to score a No 1 with 'Feel the Love' in 2012. In 2013 they teamed up with Sandé – who lived close to their London base in Hackney – on two tracks: 'Free' and 'More than Everything'. 'She came to our Brixton gig and said she really liked our music and wanted to do a track with us, and at first we didn't believe her!' Rudimental's DJ Locksmith told *Platform* magazine. 'After the Brits we got a cab down to our studio with her and we only had four hours to smash out two tracks with her vocals. She was incredible, she's such a lovely lady and such an amazing professional – there were times she was in the booth and I thought a CD was playing, she sounded that good.'

The two tracks featured on Rudimental's No 1 album *Home*. 'Free' is a tale of alienation as Sandé takes on the lyrical role of the outsider who doesn't fit in but finds freedom in the situation rather than getting down about it. There are 1960s guitar, piano, chants and a big chorus – a lost chance for a great single. 'More than Anything' is frankly brilliant – an enormous slab of quiet bit/loud bit drum'n'bass that would surely have been a massive hit if had been released as a single.

The reviewers seemed to love *Home*, especially Emeli's contributions. The *Independent* said: 'Unlike so much routine R&B hackwork, the individual components here are seamlessly combined, confirmation of the production team's strategy of having the singers involved throughout the process, rather than added as afterthoughts. This is most obviously effective in the two cuts featuring the ubiquitous Emeli Sandé, "More than Anything" and "Free", at least one of which should be a hit.'

'"More than Anything" sees Emeli at her emotive best,' said the Contact Music website, 'owning every word and belting out her soul as the beats build and break below in this tragic plea. The finale, "Free", initially strips it back for Emeli as she goes a little Tracy Chapman, but with a far more upbeat and contemporary feel complete with a brilliant dripping bass-line.

Even the *NME* – not normally the place to find a good review for Emeli – seemed to be on board: 'Emeli Sandé appears not once but twice, but don't expect to hear these tracks on Radio 2. Head for *Home* if you want to hear where drum'n'bass, dubstep, garage and old-school jungle meet in 2013, but really just pick it up if you're looking for more bangers than a barbecue at a firework factory.'

Sandé also had a two-way collaboration with American hip hop star Kendrick Lamar. First, he remixed 'Next to Me', though it sounds less like a remix and more like him rapping over the original track. 'I'm really big on songs that I like,' he told the Rap-Up video channel when asked how such an apparently unusual hook-up happened. 'I'm not big on who's doing it. I liked the song, she reached out. She's a great artist and a great vocalist and it's a great song so I just had to do it.'

'I really wanted a feature on it, something that would give the perspective of the song,' Emeli told The Boombox website. 'And I was so excited about Kendrick Lamar as an artist. He's really doing something that's so different and so honest. We approached him and asked him if it was something he'd be interested in doing and it worked out fantastic. I really love what he did on it and I'd love to work with him again.'

A few months later and the tables were turned, as Emeli appeared as a guest vocalist on Lamar's track 'Bitch, Don't Kill My Vibe'. The track had originally featured a vocal from Lady Gaga and had also had the remix treatment from Jay-Z. Emeli's vocal sounds like it was lifted from the *Have You Heard?* album as her Neo Soul singing interacts and intertwines with Kendrick's vocal and rap.

She also released an eight-track mini-album via iTunes that featured stripped-back, bare-bones versions of some of her most popular songs. These *iTunes Sessions* tracks, released in April 2013, again hark back to the Glasgow days of *Have You Heard?*, with Emeli's voice well to the fore and instrumentation kept to a bare minimum. 'Heaven' and 'Where I Sleep' get the simple voice and acoustic guitar treatment while 'Suitcase' is even simpler, with little more than a stand-up bass for accompaniment. The gospel standard 'I Wish I Knew How It Would Feel to Be Free' – recognisable to older listeners as the theme from Barry Norman's *Film* programme on the BBC – is Sandé at the piano; 'My Kind of Love', 'Clown' and 'Read All About It Pt. III' are also here in their most basic form. Only 'Next to Me' gets anything more than basic accompaniment, but that only extends to piano plus guitar.

Could these releases be indicators of where Sandé is heading? What would someone like 1Xtra's Yasmin Evans like to hear next from Emeli? 'I wouldn't want it to be "Read All About It Pt. IV", she told me. 'We've heard a lot of her ballad-type things. I'd like it to be more upbeat, something with more of a kick in it. Still working with Naughty Boy because I think he's really talented. She started off with people who are now, so to speak, "below" her in terms of being well known in the music world. When she featured on the Wiley track, it wasn't that long ago really. Now she's this huge star. She's worked with people like Professor Green and Wiley and Wretch 32: I'd like to think that she can come back around and work with them again. But maybe people will say that she's too big now, so that's gone. Because she's going upwards she can't take a step down. They were her step up at one point. Taking a step down? I don't know if this would be career-ending – but maybe going back to the kind of things she first created. Maybe going back to those first songs she never really released. Not as extravagant. Something more personal – I'd like to hear that. But a lot of people don't like change, and if they're used to Emeli Sandé, the big voice, the Olympics, they might not like it. You can't please everyone. I don't think she'll take a step back, though. Some people might say no... keep going upwards.'

Radio 1Xtra tends to get the credit when it comes to giving Emeli her earliest breaks, but as we know, BBC Radio Scotland can claim bragging rights to a large extent. BBC Scotland producer Muslim Alim, who received that early Sandé demo, is very specific about why he believes Emeli broke through. 'The first reason is the gap that Amy Winehouse left,' he explained to me. 'Amy set a precedent of a level of originality and soulfulness if you're going to do this kind of music. The second reason is that her album has a lot of break beats in it. They were making a comeback. Those are the two key elements. Plus the unusual story: black girl from Scotland.'

Muslim Alim's colleague and Urban Scot Laura McCrum – the first person to play Emeli on the radio – has believed in Emeli since she saw her stop the cleaners in their tracks at Aberdeen's Lemon Tree venue. I asked her why she thought Emeli had become so successful. 'It was never a question of why,' she told me. 'I always believed she was going to make it. When you meet such a phenomenal talent... Whether you call it God, whether you call it the universe, whether you call it cosmic energy – she's been given a gift and she's not the kind of soul who's going to abuse that. It was never a question of why for me but when.'

The only concern for McCrum was that Sandé's inherent niceness might be the only thing that could hold her back. 'If you look at who else had been on the market – Adele, Amy Winehouse, Jessie J – I remember fearing that although she had the drive she might be too polite and humble and that the chance might get taken away from her. But she could have shot to fame sooner if she'd been more aggressive. But things happen at specific times for specific reasons. It was always going to happen.'

For Richard Bull – who produced BBC Scotland's *Blackstreet* show that gave Emeli one of her earliest breaks – the Sandé niceness is actually a secret weapon. And it's a weapon she's had at her disposal since the very start when she sent her demo to the show. 'There's something appealing and friendly about her,' he explained to me. 'At the time – I never thought I'd be speaking to someone about this years later – but at the time the way her stuff was presented to us was really nicely done. She had no industry machine behind her then – it was just a family thing. There's something of that about her now – something approachable and unpretentious. I'd like to think that at some level, quality wins the day – and I know that doesn't always happen. There's something intergenerational about her as well, isn't there? It's middle-aged people, kids, people Emeli's age, older people... she's not a niche artist and I don't think that's happened by marketing, I think that's just the way she is. She can appear with Professor Green and she can sing a hymn at the Olympics.'

That appeal extends to her fellow artists too – many musicians and singers hold Sandé in high esteem, and they couldn't be more varied. Emeli collaborator Wiley, the man behind her breakout track 'Never Be Your Woman': 'Listen to this,' he told Digital Spy. 'I rate her more than Adele. I like Adele but I rate Emeli more. Adele is sick but Emeli is against [the] odds. A lot of people thought she wouldn't go anywhere and she did. I didn't think England would accept her.' Soul legend Ruby Turner: 'I've been very impressed with how Emeli has dealt with her success and I think she is terrific,' she told STV. 'I met her in Finland, and she was amazing, very down-to-earth, but full of passion for what she was doing and she struck me as a major talent. Some people get carried away with success and being in the media, but Emeli hasn't let it affect her. I bought her debut album [*Our Version of Events*] and it was clear from listening to the songs that she wasn't some pre-packaged star, but the genuine article. She is intelligent, she does things her own way, and she walks her own path. In many ways, she reminded me of the [US singer] Anita Baker and that is no small recommendation.' Multi-million selling singer Dido: 'I think she's brilliant,' she told the *Daily Mail*. 'It's voices that resonate with me, and I love hers. She's the most exciting female artist of the moment. She never gets boring, either, because I don't know anything about her private life, which is great.'

Sandé herself – a most unlikely pop star, as she describes herself – seems slightly overawed not only by her success but by the admiration of her peers. 'I try and think of how, if I went back and told 14-year-old me what's going on now, I don't think she'd quite believe it,' she told the *Liverpool Echo*. 'It's really incredible, and very surreal when people that you've looked up to for so long appreciate you as an artist, and respect you as well, it's an incredible feeling.'

Sandé seems to bring out the best in others too – right through her story there have been people wanting to go out of their way to help her. From the very start there was the obvious and constant support of her parents – Joel Sandé and his ever-present video camera at every gig from school concerts to the Royal Albert Hall was clearly a major influence. He now believes that it's his daughter's turn to be a good influence: 'I think she can be a very positive role model,' he told the *Sunday Times*. 'A good example of what can come out of somebody who works hard and puts their mind to something. And also that coming from a small place like Alford needn't prevent anybody from trying hard and doing something better in the world.'

Then there was John Ansdell and his family putting money into her early career and then the assistance and support of the Urban Scot team: everyone seemed to want to help Emeli get to where she wanted to be. Her manager Adrian Sykes – the man who took a plane to Aberdeen to meet Emeli when she was still at school – was so convinced he was the man to help Emeli make it, he was prepared to wait for six years. He has his own recipe for Sandé's success: 'Nurturing the career is also nurturing the person,' he told the hitquarters website. 'You allow the artist the space to make the record they want to make and prevent them from being stressed by what happens within the confines of a record company. It's important to maintain relationships with the record company guys and listen to what they have to say, but at the same time you have to be creatively happy with what you're doing – there's nothing worse than compromising what you do in order to be successful. Whatever happens you've always got to try to keep creative control because at least then you can still always hold your head up high and say, "I did it my way." That might sound a little clichéd but it really is very, very important. There's always artists who'll look back over their career and say, "You know what? I wish I'd done it differently." Invest yourself emotionally and you'll get more out of it. Because if you believe in what you are doing, you can sell it in a believable way.'

But none of this would mean anything without the songs. From the start no one seems to have been in any doubt about their quality – seek out 'Baby's Eyes', the great 'lost' song from the early days that so many interviewees have raved about. As we've seen, Sandé could now be making a perfectly good living as a songwriter and no one outside the inner workings of the music industry would know her name. But it's putting in the time as songwriter for others that Sandé believes made her into the artist she is today. 'Working for other people was a great learning curve for me, because it really made me understand the music industry,' she told AllHipHop. 'It made me understand radio. It also made me see that when working with different artists and just seeing how different teams work, unless you specifically know what you want to say, other people are going to decide for you. That, for me, was like, before I even attempt to be an artist, I need to know exactly what I want to say and what type of artist I want to be. I think more than anything, you need to understand the industry. But seeing other people sing my work is great because the way I write is an emotional way of writing and I'm always very honest no matter if the song is for me or for somebody else. So, when I see people interpret what I'm singing, they're usually interpreting it in a way that's emotional for them. They're never faking it. So, I love seeing different people's interpretations. They found something in their life or their emotions that is connected with that song. It's always interesting for me to see that.' Beyond the big hooks and the impassioned delivery, there might be something else: Sandé's lyrics seem to strike a chord with people – largely perhaps because they are unusually upbeat.

She clearly sees herself in terms of the values and credentials belonging to musicians and singers of the past, rather than her contemporaries. The names she drops are largely from the 20th century, rather than the 21st. 'When I was a kid, I looked up to Nina Simone. I know that I will never play piano like her, but I am going to try. Her lyrics are so poetic. So when I listen to commercial stuff at the moment, I'm just thinking, haven't you heard Nina Simone, haven't you heard how a song should be written? I can only hope that my songs can last as hers do. A lot of the songs these days are for the moment. They make us feel good and we can dance to them, but the poetry has been lost in the lyric. Great songwriters come along quite rarely, but when I listen to Tracy Chapman or Joni Mitchell – these are people who pay attention to the lyric and are precise about it. I feel that has been put second to having a cool producer or whether the kids will like it. People think they can be songwriters because they're singers, but it's an art. You need to work on your voice, but also you must understand reading a lyric. I am working on it.'

The other thing that marks Sandé out is her unwillingness to 'play the game' in celebrity terms. If she is in the press it's because of an event, an achievement or a release – not because she's falling out of a nightclub or lacking in clothing. There was a time when she wasn't even willing to use her husband's name in the press, let alone sell their wedding pictures to the highest bidder. She may not seek attention, but it often comes her way anyway. 'That's something that I'm still getting used to,' she told Clare Balding in an interview on the BBC. 'Naturally I feel like a musician and I could do that all day and every day. The type of music I put out and the message I'm trying to put out isn't about being famous or being a celebrity, so when I do meet people on the street they're always really respectful and speak to me about songs on the album or lyrics. I really enjoy that: you get a real sense of what people are thinking and feeling.'

But being famous comes with the territory when you've reached the level of success that Sandé has now attained. She's now on the rich list for young performers in the UK and her US success can only push her further up the cash charts. Success can drain the hunger and creativity from an artist – something

Sandé seems very aware of. 'If I became distracted by the trappings of success, my music would suffer and change,' she told the audience at the launch of an American fund to offer scholarships for young musicians. 'It would become something that wasn't important any more, because you're just speaking about yourself.'

Sandé's Scottishness is key here – the Urban Scot from a village in Aberdeenshire seems to display levels of good sense and caution that border on a Caledonian caricature. The Scottish media treat Emeli as being almost untouchable – woe betide anyone south of the border who criticises their girl. But as far as the Scottish music scene is concerned, Emeli may not pass the cool test any more. *Our Version of Events* was left off the shortlist for Scottish Album of the Year – Calvin Harris suffered the same fate – in favour of albums by Twilight Sad, Admiral Fallow, Django Django, Stanley Odd and Meursault.

Perhaps Sandé doesn't need the cool approval of others to validate what she's doing – maybe in her version of events, there are different reasons for her to be a musician. 'The way I hope I stand out is through my work,' she once said. 'I wrote the way I wrote and I think that's quite unique to me. I don't think it can be copied really. What I think I can bring is something that's really honest. I hope I can represent black females as well in the industry. We can create something that is art. It doesn't have to be sexy all the time, it doesn't have to be loud all the time. We can be great writers and we can be intelligent in what we do.'

Twelve

Discography, DVDs,
key songwriting credits
and collaborations

This is the first Emeli Sandé discography to include the material she recorded as Adele Sandé and her recordings with Souljawn and Starla Records before she signed to Virgin.

ALBUMS

Have You Heard? (as Adele Sandé) – CD, Souljawn Records, 2007
'Best Friend'
'Baby's Eyes'
'Has Needs'
'Silent'
'Dirty Jeans & Sweater'
'Patchwork'

'Your Song'
'Woman's Touch' (live at the BBC)

Have You Heard? (as Adele Sandé) – Digital EP, Souljawn Records, 2008
'Best Friend'
'Baby's Eyes'
'Has Needs'
'Your Song'

Our Version of Events – CD/Download, Virgin Records, 2012
'Heaven'
'My Kind of Love'
'Where I Sleep'
'Mountains'
'Clown'
'Daddy' (featuring Naughty Boy)
'Maybe'
'Suitcase'
'Breaking the Law'
'Next to Me'
'River'
'Lifetime'
'Hope'
'Read All About It (Pt. III)' [bonus track]

Our Version of Events – Special Edition, Virgin Records, 2012
As above plus:
'Wonder' (Naughty Boy featuring Emeli Sandé)
'Breaking the Law' (alternate version)
'Easier in Bed'

'Imagine'
'Beneath Your Beautiful' (Labrinth featuring Emeli Sandé)

Additional iTunes track
'Tiger'

Emeli Sandé Live at the Royal Albert Hall – CD/MP3/DVD, Virgin Records, 2013
Disc 1 (CD)
'Daddy'
'Where I Sleep'
'Breaking the Law'
'Enough'
'My Kind of Love'
'Clown'
'River'
'I Wish I Knew How It Would Feel to Be Free'
'Suitcase'
'Read All About It (Pt. III)' (featuring Professor Green)
'Wonder'
'Mountains'
'Heaven'
'Beneath Your Beautiful' (featuring Labrinth)
'Maybe'
'Next to Me'

Disc 2 (DVD)
'Daddy'
'Tiger'
'Where I Sleep'
'Breaking the Law'

'Enough'
'Pluto' (featuring The Heroes)
'My Kind of Love'
'Abide With Me'
'Clown'
'River'
'I Wish I Knew How It Would Feel to Be Free'
'Suitcase'
'Read All About It (Pt. III)' (featuring Professor Green)
'Wonder'
'Mountains'
'Heaven'
'Beneath Your Beautiful' (featuring Labrinth)
'Maybe'
'Next to Me'

Emeli Sandé iTunes Sessions – US download, Virgin
Records, 2013
'Heaven'
'Where I Sleep'
'Suitcase'
'I Wish I Knew How It Would Feel to Be Free'
'My Kind of Love'
'Next to Me'
'Clown'
'Read All About It (Pt. III)'

SINGLES (as the main artist)

'Heaven' – Virgin Records, 2011
1 'Heaven'

2 'Heaven' (Instrumental)
3 'Heaven' (Live from Angel Studios)
4 'Easier in Bed' (Acoustic Version)
5 'Kill the Boy' (Live from Angel Studios)

'Heaven (Remixes EP)' – Virgin Records, 2011
1 'Heaven' (Nu:Tone Remix)
2 'Heaven' (We Don't Belong In Pacha Remix)
3 'Heaven' (Mojam Remix)
4 'Heaven' (Stripped)

'Daddy' (featuring Naughty Boy) – single and digital remixes, Virgin Records, 2012
1 'Daddy'
2 'Daddy' (Fred V and Grafix Remix)
3 'Daddy' (Disclosure Remix)
4 'Daddy' (Third Party Remix)
5 'Daddy' (Cyantific Remix)
6 'Daddy' (Ifan Dafydd Remix)

'Next to Me' – single and digital remixes, Virgin Records, 2012
1 'Next to Me'
2 'Next to Me' (Nu:Tone Remix)
3 'Next to Me' (Mojam Remix)
4 'Next to Me' (Dorian Remix)
5 'Next to Me' (Nu:Tone Dub)
6 'Next to Me' (Next to Me in Bed Remix)

'Next to Me' – US Remix EP, Virgin Records, 2013
1 'Next to Me' (MOTi Remix)
2 'Next to Me' (James Egbert Mixshow Edit)

3 'Next to Me' (Manhattan Clique Mixshow Edit)
4 'Next to Me' (MOTi BrightLight Mixshow Edit)

'My Kind of Love' – single and digital remixes, Virgin Records, 2012
1 'My Kind of Love' (Radio Mix)
2 'My Kind of Love' (Live from Hollywood)
3 'My Kind of Love' (Gemini Remix)
4 'My Kind of Love' (Machinedrum Remix)
5 'My Kind of Love' (Wideboys Remix)

'Clown' – single and digital EP, Virgin Records, 2013
1 'Clown'
2 'Clown' (Live at the Royal Albert Hall)
3 'Kill the Boy'
4 'Clown' (Instrumental)
5 'Clown' (Music video)

STANDALONE DIGITAL DOWNLOADS

'Abide With Me', 2012
'Read All About It (Pt. III)', 2012

SINGLES (as a featuring artist)

'Takes' – Emeli Sandé & Marco with The DT6, 7 inch single, B-side of '(Theme From) The Baden Persuader', Starla Records, 2009
'Diamond Rings' – Chipmunk featuring Emeli Sandé, Virgin Records, 2009
'Never Be Your Woman' – Naughty Boy presents Wiley

featuring Emeli Sandé, Virgin Records, 2010

'Read All About It' – Professor Green featuring Emeli Sandé, Virgin Records, 2011

'Wonder' – Naughty Boy featuring Emeli Sandé, Virgin Records, 2012

'Beneath Your Beautiful' – Labrinth featuring Emeli Sandé, Syco, 2012

ADDITIONAL TRACKS (as a featuring artist)

'Kids That Love to Dance' – Professor Green featuring Emeli Sandé, from the album *Alive Till I'm Dead*, Virgin Records, 2010

'Dreamer' – Devlin featuring Emeli Sandé, from the album *Bud, Sweat and Beers*, Island/Universal, 2011, Virgin Records, 2010

'Underdog Law' – Wretch 32 & Emeli Sandé, free download, 2011

'Free'/'More Than Everything' – Rudimental featuring Emeli Sandé, from the album *Home*, Asylum, 2013

'Here It Comes' – Emeli Sandé and Rick Smith, original soundtrack from the film *Trance*, 2013

'Crazy in Love' – Emeli Sandé and The Bryan Ferry Orchestra, original soundtrack from the film *The Great Gatsby*, Polydor, 2013

'Next to Me' (Remix) – Emeli Sandé featuring Kendrick Lamar, 2013

'Bitch, Don't Kill My Vibe' (Remix) – Kendrick Lamar featuring Emeli Sandé, 2013

CO-SONGWRITING AND LYRIC CREDITS (NOT INCLUDING SOLO AND FEATURED ARTIST RELEASES)

'Boys' – single B-side, Cheryl Cole, Fascination, 2009

'Let Go' – album track, Tinie Tempah, Parlophone, 2009

'Til the End' – Tinchy Stryder, album track from *Third Strike*, Takeover/Universal, 2009

'Radio' – single, Alesha Dixon, Asylum, 2010

'Brainwashed'/'Yesterdays News'/'Dreamer' – album tracks *from Bud, Sweat and Beers*, Devlin, Island/Universal, 2010

'Find a Boy' – promotional single, A*M*E featuring Mic Righteous, Future, 2010

'Let It Rain' – single, Tinchy Stryder featuring Melanie Fiona, Takeover/Universal, 2011

'Avalon' – single, Professor Green featuring Sierra Kusterbeck, Virgin Records, 2011

'This Will Be the Year' – album track from *Someone to Watch Over Me*, Susan Boyle, Syco, 2011

'Rokstar' – album track from *Parade*, Parade, Asylum, 2011

'Trouble'/'I to You'/'Sugar' – album tracks from *Glassheart*, Leona Lewis, Syco, 2012

'Half of Me' – additional track from album *Unapologetic*, Rihanna, Def Jam, 2012

'Not Even the King'/'Brand New Me'/'101' – album tracks from *Girl on Fire*, Alicia Keys, RCA, 2012

'Side Effects of You' – album track from *Side Effects of You*, Fantasia, RCA, 2013